After Lermontov

Mikhail Lermontov (1814–41 ....
speaking readers as the author c ....
among Russian readers his poetr ....ursting
into print with an impassioned p. .... on the death of Pushkin,
he continued to attract unfavourable attention from the author-
ities while enjoying a high reputation in literary circles and
beyond. Although he declared in one poem that he was 'not
Byron', he was greatly influenced by his reading of Byron and
of Walter Scott. His autobiographical lyrics and longer poems
could be labelled as Romantic, Brodsky maintains, were it not
for Lermontov's 'thoroughly corrosive self-knowledge'. Having
served in the Caucasus, and taken part in dangerous engage-
ments against the Chechens, like Pushkin he died in a duel of
dubious legality.

Peter France was Professor of French at the University of Edin-
burgh from 1980 to 2000. He has written many studies of
French and Russian literature (including *Poets of Modern Russia*,
1982), and is the editor of the *Oxford Guide to Literature in English
Translation* and general editor of the five-volume *Oxford History
of Literary Translation in English*. He has translated French and
Russian prose texts as well as several volumes of Russian poetry
– Blok and Pasternak (with Jon Stallworthy), Mayakovsky, and
in particular Gennady Aygi, including *Selected Poems 1954–
1994*, *Child-and-Rose*, *Salute – to Singing*, *Field-Russia*, and most
recently *Winter Revels*. He is currently preparing volumes of
translations of Baratynsky and of Mandelstam.

Robyn Marsack has been Director of the Scottish Poetry Library
in Edinburgh since 2000, and has facilitated many poetry
translation workshops in partnership with Literature Across
Frontiers. She was formerly a publishers' editor, working for
Carcanet Press and then freelance, also as a critic and translator.
She translated Nina Berberova's *Aleksandr Blok: A Life*, and has
co-edited several poetry anthologies, including *Intimate
Expanses: XXV Scottish Poems 1978–2002* and *Twenty Contem-
porary New Zealand Poets*.

Russian poetry available from Carcanet Press

Aleksandr Blok, *Selected Poems*, translated by Jon Stallworthy
    and Peter France
Joseph Brodsky, *Collected Poems in English*, edited by Anne
    Kjellberg and translated by Anthony Hecht
Natalya Gorbanevskaya, *Selected Poems*, translated by Daniel
    Weissbort
Marina Tsvetaeva, *Bride of Ice: Selected Poems*, translated by
    Elaine Feinstein
An Anthology of Contemporary Russian Women Poets, edited by
    Daniel Weissbort and Valentina Polukhina
What I Own: Versions of Hölderlin and Mandelshtam, edited and
    translated by John Riley and Tim Longville

After Lermontov
Translations for the Bicentenary

Edited by Peter France and Robyn Marsack

CARCANET

in association with the Scottish Poetry Library

First published in Great Britain in 2014 by
Carcanet Press Limited
Alliance House
Cross Street
Manchester M2 7AQ

www.carcanet.co.uk

in association with
The Scottish Poetry Library
5 Crichton's Close
Edinburgh EH8 8DT

www.scottishpoetrylibrary.org.uk

Translations copyright © the individual translators 2014
Introduction copyright © Peter France 2014

The right of Peter France and Robyn Marsack to be identified as
the editors of this work has been asserted by them in accordance with
the Copyright, Designs and Patents Act of 1988

All rights reserved

A CIP catalogue record for this book is available from the British Library

ISBN 978 1 84777 275 6

The publishers gratefully acknowledge financial support from
Arts Council England, the Institute of Translation (Russia)
and Dr David Summers Charitable Trust.

Typeset by XL Publishing Services, Exmouth
Printed and bound in England by SRP Ltd, Exeter

Acknowledgements

The idea for this set of new translations of Lermontov arose during a visit by Dr Ekaterina Genieva, Director of the Russian State Library for Foreign Literature (VGBIL), to Moffat in Dumfries and Galloway, where she was the guest of Elizabeth Roberts, co-founder of Moffat Book Events (MBE). MBE, a Scottish charity, is partnered by VGBIL in a programme of literary and other cultural projects in Scotland and Russia. See www.moffatbookevents.co.uk.

The project was developed under Peter France's editorship, with the assistance of Robyn Marsack, Director of the Scottish Poetry Library. The editors wish to thank Dr Genieva and Dr Evgeny Reznichenko, Director of the Institute of Translation (Russia), for their encouragement, Rose France for providing literal translations of Lermontov's poems and the poets themselves for their willingness to give Lermontov new life in English and Scots.

Содержание

Contents

Introduction

Balcomie Castle towers among trees, just outside the fishing village of Crail in the East Neuk of Fife, looking out over the North Sea. This grand sixteenth-century house was the home of an ancient Scottish family, the Learmonths; from here one George Learmonth set off at the beginning of the seventeenth century to seek a fortune as a soldier in the troubled land of Muscovy. And it was to this Scottish adventurer – and before him to the semi-legendary Thomas Learmonth, Thomas the Rhymer – that Mikhail Lermontov traced his ancestry. His youthful poem, 'A Wish', speaks of his desire to fly away, raven-like, to his native wild place, an empty castle in misty mountains. It is clear that the poet's romantic vision of Scotland was fed by literary sources – Ossian and Walter Scott – and this vision may in its turn have influenced the way he saw the region with which he is most associated, the Caucasus. Another Scot, Byron – generally not perceived as Scottish outside Scotland – bulked large in the pantheon of the young Lermontov.

For these reasons, Lermontov could be seen as one of the most Scottish of Russian writers (he is certainly one of the most Russian). But although there is a thriving association that brings together the Learmonth and Lermontov families, it cannot be said that the poet has been given a particularly important place in Scottish culture. In particular, Scottish poets have not rushed to translate him. It is true that the first English translation of one of his writings ('The Gifts of Terek', translated by the Englishman Thomas Budge Shaw) was published in an Edinburgh magazine, *Blackwood's*, but in the twentieth century he figured only rarely in Scottish journals. Nor does his work seem to have tempted the two great Scottish poet-translators, Edwin Morgan and Alastair Mackie, both of whom were very open to Russian poetry. The present volume, made in Edinburgh for the bicentenary of the poet's birth in 2014, aims to give Lermontov a more prominent place in Scottish literary culture.

★

Mikhail Yurievich Lermontov was born in Moscow in October

1814; his father was a retired army captain, the descendant of George Learmonth. After his mother's death in 1817 he was taken off by his possessive maternal grandmother to her estate in central Russia, where he spent the next ten years, receiving an excellent education, and developing his precocious talents as writer and artist (he left an impressive body of graphic work: sharply executed caricatures, scenes of military life, landscapes). As a boy and a young man, he made several visits to the Caucasus, where the mountain scenery and primitive life made a deep impression on him.

In 1827 he moved to Moscow, where he attended first a private school and then Moscow University. During these years he wrote great quantities of poetry, much of it inspired by unhappy love affairs. Leaving university after a conflict with the authorities, he transferred to a military academy in St Petersburg, graduating in 1834, when he received a commission in the Life Guard Hussars. As a young officer, he acquired a reputation as a debauchee, a dandy and a cynical wit. He continued to write, both prose and verse, and in 1837 attained instant fame with the poem 'On the Death of a Poet', a passionately rhetorical denunciation of those responsible for Pushkin's death in a duel. Since this touched on circles close to the Tsar, Lermontov was arrested, tried, and punished by being sent to serve as a Dragoons officer in the Caucasus.

A year later he was pardoned and returned to the capital, by now a celebrity. He frequented high society and joined literary circles, including a secret political debating society; his poetry appeared regularly in literary journals, and in 1840 he published two volumes of verse and a work of prose fiction, *A Hero of Our Time*. Early the same year he had fought a bloodless duel with the son of the French ambassador, as a result of which he was sent back to the Caucasus. This time he served in a line regiment, taking part in dangerous engagements against the Chechens and other mountain peoples such as the one described so vividly in 'Valerik'. He was put up for awards for bravery, but the recommendations were turned down by the authorities, Lermontov being regarded with suspicion and hostility by Tsar Nicholas and his police chief.

The following year Lermontov went to take the waters at

Pyatigorsk in the northern Caucasus. In 'A Dream', he had vividly imagined his own death in a duel in the Caucasus, and so it was to be, possibly with the connivance of the highest authorities. His former friend N.S. Martynov, for reasons that remain uncertain, challenged him and shot him dead in a rainstorm, in apparently suspicious circumstances, on 15 July 1841. His death echoed that of Pushkin four years earlier, but there was no one to write 'On the Death of a Poet' for him.

In a short life, Lermontov wrote a great deal. He was the author of several plays, the most successful being *The Masquerade*, with its characteristically world-weary hero. This hero figure was further developed, but in a much more subtle way, in Lermontov's best-known work (the only one widely known in the West), *A Hero of Our Time*; this is usually described as a novel, though it is really a series of tales linked by the central character, Pechorin. There are several other prose narratives, some of them unfinished; 'Ashik-Kerib', a Turkish tale, provided the subject for a remarkable film by the Armenian film director Paradzhanov. And there are an equally large number of extended verse narratives, notably 'Mtsyri' (translated as 'The Novice' by Charles Johnston), and the two masterpieces which are represented by excerpts in the present volume, the 'Song of the Tsar Ivan Vaslilyevich...' and 'The Demon'. The first is a magnificent recreation or pastiche of the folk epics known as *byliny*, sung to the stringed instrument called the *gusli*. The second, which has become virtually synonymous with Lermontov in Russia, is an 'Eastern Tale'; the fallen angel of the title falls in love with a village beauty, she pities him, but dies of his kiss, and he remains a damned spirit roaming the earth. The poem was begun in 1829 and probably finished ten years later, by which time Lermontov had enriched it with captivating pictures of the wild Caucasus. It later inspired some famous works by the artist Mikhail Vrubel.

As for the shorter poems, with which this volume is mainly concerned, there is a mass of lyric verse written before the age of 20 and not included by Lermontov in his published poems. These poems are usually seen as prentice work, derivative Romantic pieces, Byronic in attitude in spite of the poet's disclaimers. They are often wonderfully musical, however, and some of them, such as 'Angel' and 'Sail', have become great popular favourites, often set to music and recited by heart. A relatively small selection from this early work will be found here, including poems which dwell on the poet's Scottish ancestry.

By general agreement, Lermontov's essential poetic achievements date from the four years between his emergence as a public poet in 1837 and his death in 1841. In many cases, these poems develop the personal lyricism of his early verse, but with a new power and originality ('It's dull and it's sad...', 'Night-Walk'). A good number of them pursue the political, satirical line of 'On the Death of a Poet'; Lermontov was not detached from contemporary life, and he was not unwilling to come out fighting. 'Journalist, Reader and Writer' reflects in a Pushkinian way on the possibilities of poetry in the modern age, and other poems attack a variety of targets, from the falsities of polite society ('Never trust yourself') to the oppressions of the tsarist regime ('Unwasht Russia, fare ye weel') or the hypocrisy of bourgeois France bringing back Napoleon's remains to a hero's burial ('The Final Welcome Home'). Particularly remarkable is the way this most self-centred of poets manages to project himself into the minds of others, to adopt a voice far remote from his own, as in 'Borodino' and 'Last Will'. In one case, the long poem 'Valerik', the romantic passion of the poet serves as a frame for a stunningly realistic rendering of an early Chechen war, a verse anticipation of the *Sebastopol Stories* that Tolstoy would write some fifteen years later.

Having shot to fame in 1837, Lermontov was widely regarded as Russia's greatest living poet, the true heir of Pushkin, and he was to remain an undoubted popular favourite. But his brief poetic career can also be seen as the swan-song of the great age of Russian poetry, the Golden Age which was dealt a mortal blow by the death of Pushkin. After Lermontov in his turn had been killed, there were still to be major volumes of verse by Evgeny Baratynsky and Fedor Tyutchev, but poetry, after its gorgeous flourishing, had been displaced by prose as the driving force of Russian literary culture. Pushkin himself had increasingly preferred prose, and Lermontov, with *A Hero of Our Time*, had gone one step further in the creation of modern Russian prose fiction. It is all the more remarkable that at the same time he was writing some of the greatest poems in the Russian language.

★

This bilingual Scottish edition of Lermontov's poems is meant to be read in the English-speaking world, but also in countries where Russian is spoken and where readers are interested in seeing how Lermontov fares in English or Scots translation. A bilingual volume takes up more space, so the editors have had to be quite selective. As well as two excerpts from longer poems, we have included many of Lermontov's best-known shorter poems, and a few from his voluminous juvenilia. The poems are arranged in rough chronological order, except that we begin with the opening sections of 'The Demon' (on which he worked from 1829 to about 1840).

The translations are all new, made especially for this volume. They are the work of sixteen translator-poets, some of whom know Russian, while others have worked from annotated literal versions, generally trying out their results on Russian speakers. We haven't attempted to impose a uniform style of translating, since the variety of responses provoked by Lermontov is an essential part of our story. But whether they are close or free, whether or not they aim to echo the form of the Russian, they are all *translations*, fixing their attention on the original work with a view to making it live again in English or in Scots. Almost all the translators are Scots by birth or by residence, but the majority translate in English. We are very glad, though, to be able to include a number of poems in Scots, hoping that these will show what a good medium the old language is for the translation of a poet who very likely did not know of its existence. For one short poem, 'Unwasht Russia, fare ye weel', we have printed translations into both Scots and English.

Peter France
Edinburgh, October 2013

After Lermontov

Translations for the Bicentenary

Демон: Восточная повесть
(Часть 1, 1–9)

1

Печальный Демон, дух изгнанья,
Летал над грешною землей,
И лучших дней воспоминанья
Пред ним теснилися толпой;
Тех дней, когда в жилище света
Блистал он, чистый херувим,
Когда бегущая комета
Улыбкой ласковой привета
Любила поменяться с ним,
Когда сквозь вечные туманы,
Познанья жадный, он следил
Кочующие караваны
В пространстве брошенных светил;
Когда он верил и любил,
Счастливый первенец творенья!
Не знал ни злобы, ни сомненья.
И не грозил уму его
Веков бесплодных ряд унылый…
И много, много… и всего
Припомнить не имел он силы!

2

Давно отверженный блуждал
В пустыне мира без приюта:
Вослед за веком век бежал,
Как за минутою минута,
Однообразной чередой.
Ничтожной властвуя землей,
Он сеял зло без наслажденья.
Нигде искусству своему
Он не встречал сопротивленья –
И зло наскучило ему.

The Demon: An Eastern Tale
(Part I, 1–9)

1

A mournful demon, outcast spirit,
Flew high above the sinful earth,
And in a multitude the memories
Of better days came swarming forth;
Of those days when in radiant halls
He shone, a perfect child of light,
And when the fiery comet, racing
Across the heavens would love to hail him,
Exchanging smiles of fond delight,
When through wreaths of mist eternal,
Thirsty for knowledge, he had traced
The paths of caravans that wandered
Across the vast celestial wastes;
When he had still known love and faith,
Blessed first-born of creation!
To evil and to doubt a stranger,
His mind untroubled by the round
Of fruitless ages without number;
And more – and so much more, besides
That it still pained him to remember.

2

The outcast had long roamed this world,
Which seemed to him a hostile desert:
Age after age had flown by, just
As minute follows after minute,
In a monotonous parade.
Over the wretched world he reigned,
Sowed evil with a weary heart,
And nowhere did he meet his equal
Or find resistance to his art –
And he grew tired of doing evil.

И над вершинами Кавказа
Изгнанник рая пролетал:
Под ним Казбек, как грань алмаза,
Снегами вечными сиял,
И, глубоко внизу чернея,
Как трещина, жилище змея,
Вился излучистый Дарьял,
И Терек, прыгая, как львица
С косматой гривой на хребте,
Ревел, — и горный зверь и птица,
Кружась в лазурной высоте,
Глаголу вод его внимали;
И золотые облака
Из южных стран, издалека
Его на север провожали;
И скалы тесною толпой,
Таинственной дремоты полны,
Над ним склонялись головой,
Следя мелькающие волны;
И башни замков на скалах
Смотрели грозно сквозь туманы —
У врат Кавказа на часах
Сторожевые великаны!
И дик и чуден был вокруг
Весь божий мир; но гордый дух
Презрительным окинул оком
Творенье бога своего,
И на челе его высоком
Не отразилось ничего.

И перед ним иной картины
Красы живые расцвели:
Роскошной Грузии долины
Ковром раскинулись вдали;

Over the Caucasus' steep ridges
Flew heaven's outcast; down below
Like a raw diamond, Kazbek glittered,
White with the everlasting snow,
And deep beneath it, black with menace,
Like some great serpent's rocky crevice,
The Darial wound its tortuous road.
The Terek, like a lioness bounding,
Maned with a shaggy crest of white,
Roared – and the beasts upon the mountain,
The eagles in the azure heights,
All heard the message of its waters;
And golden clouds that made their way
From southern lands, from far away,
Followed it as it travelled northwards.
And crags that clustered in dense throngs
All heavy with mysterious slumber
Bent their great heads to look upon
The gleaming ripples of the river.
And on the crags the castle towers
Watched ominously through the mists.
Like giant sentries, set to guard
The gateway to the Caucasus.
Before him, wonderful and wild
Was all God's earth; but, full of pride,
He cast a scornful eye about him,
At everything his God had made,
And not a shadow of emotion
Was on his lofty brow betrayed.

4

And then beneath him a new vision
Revealed itself in colours bright;
A fertile Georgian valley, spreading
Like a rich carpet, far and wide;

Счастливый, пышный край земли!
Столпообразные раины.
Звонко-бегущие ручьи
По дну из камней разноцветных,
И кущи роз, где соловьи
Поют красавиц, безответных
На сладкий голос их любви;
Чинар развесистые сени,
Густым венчанные плющом.
Пещеры, где палящим днем
Таятся робкие олени;
И блеск, и жизнь, и шум листов,
Стозвучный говор голосов,
Дыханье тысячи растений!
И полдня сладострастный зной,
И ароматною росой
Всегда увлаженные ночи,
И звезды, яркие, как очи,
Как взор грузинки молодой!..
Но, кроме зависти холодной,
Природы блеск не возбудил
В груди изгнанника бесплодной
Ни новых чувств, ни новых сил;
И все, что пред собой он видел,
Он презирал иль ненавидел.

5

Высокий дом, широкий двор
Седой Гудал себе построил…
Трудов и слез он много стоил
Рабам послушным с давних пор.
С утра на скат соседних гор
От стен его ложатся тени.
В скале нарублены ступени;
Они от башни угловой
Ведут к реке, по ним мелькая,
Покрыта белою чадрой,

Abundant land, most happy sight!
With poplars straight and tall as pillars
And brightly echoing streams that glide
On jewelled beds of stones, and bowers
Of roses, where the nightingales
Still serenade unheeding beauties
In the sweet voice of love's delight.
The sycamore's wide-spreading branches
Crowned with dense ivy, and the caves
Where, in the scorching heat of day,
The timid deer conceal themselves
The dazzle, life and noise of leaves;
The chorus of a hundred voices,
The breathing of a thousand flowers!
The sensual swelter of the midday;
And the warm nights that follow, bathed
In the refreshing dewfall fragrant,
And stars as bright as eyes, resplendent
As a young Georgian maiden's gaze;
But save a feeling of cold envy
Nature's beauty could arouse
In the heart of that barren outcast
No fresh emotion, no fresh powers;
And everything before his eyes
He either hated or despised.

5

A tall house and a spacious court
Gudal had built upon the mountain,
By years of toil and tears of countless
Humble servants dearly bought;
At dawn the neighbouring mountains caught
Its shadow on their craggy slopes
Hewn from the cliff, a flight of steps
Led from the corner tower; each day
Along those steps to the Aragva
Her head swathed in a snowy veil,

Княжна Тамара молодая
К Арагве ходит за водой.

6

Всегда безмолвно на долины
Глядел с утеса мрачный дом;
Но пир большой сегодня в нем –
Звучит зурна, и льются вины –
Гудал сосватал дочь свою,
На пир он созвал всю семью.
На кровле, устланной коврами,
Сидит невеста меж подруг:
Средь игр и песен их досуг
Проходит. Дальними горами
Уж спрятан солнца полукруг;
В ладони мерно ударяя,
Они поют – и бубен свой
Берет невеста молодая.
И вот она, одной рукой
Кружа его над головой,
То вдруг помчится легче птицы,
То остановится, глядит –
И влажный взор ее блестит
Из-под завистливой ресницы;
То черной бровью поведет,
То вдруг наклонится немножко,
И по ковру скользит, плывет
Ее божественная ножка;
И улыбается она,
Веселья детского полна.
Но луч луны, по влаге зыбкой
Слегка играющий порой,
Едва ль сравнится с той улыбкой,
Как жизнь, как молодость, живой.

Princess Tamara to the river
With water pitcher made her way.

6

For long years that bleak house in silence
Had looked down from the precipice;
But this day it would host a feast:
The *zurna* played and wine was flowing –
Today the princess would be wed
And Gudal all his clan had called
To join the revels. The rooftop terrace
Was strewn with carpets. There the bride
Sat with her friends, in song they whiled
Away the hours. And now, half-hidden
The sun behind the peaks descends,
Then clapping out a steady rhythm,
They start to sing – the young bride stands,
And with a movement deft and sudden
She takes her tambourine in hand.
She circles it above her head
Then, swiftly as a small bird flitting,
Darts to one side, then stops her dance
And now a molten, lustrous glance
Beneath her jealous lashes glitters;
And now she arches her dark brow;
Now makes a sudden, graceful bow
And light across the carpet, now,
Her heavenly feet go tripping, gliding;
And then she smiles a smile so bright,
So full of innocent delight,
A moonbeam on the ripples shining
Soft lifted by the swelling tide,
Could not compare with that sweet smiling,
As radiant as youth, or life.

Клянусь полночною звездой,
Лучом заката и востока,
Властитель Персии златой
И ни единый царь земной
Не целовал такого ока;
Гарема брызжущий фонтан
Ни разу жаркою порою
Своей жемчужною росою
Не омывал подобный стан!
Еще ничья рука земная,
По милому челу блуждая,
Таких волос не расплела;
Стех пор как мир лишился рая,
Клянусь, красавица такая
Под солнцем юга не цвела.

В последний раз она плясала.
Увы! заутра ожидала
Ее, наследницу Гудала.
Свободы резвую дитя,
Судьба печальная рабыни,
Отчизна, чуждая поныне,
И незнакомая семья.
И часто тайное сомненье
Темнило светлые черты;
И были все ее движенья
Так стройны, полны выраженья,
Так полны милой простоты,
Что если б Демон, пролетая,
В то время на нее взглянул,
То, прежних братий вспоминая,
Он отвернулся б – и вздохнул…

7

I swear upon the midnight star
The sunset and the morning radiance,
Neither the golden ruler of far
Persia, nor any earthly Tsar
Had ever kissed an eye so beauteous
And, in the southern summer's warmth,
The fountain in the harem courtyard
In sparkling streams of dewy water
Had never bathed so fine a form.
No mortal hand yet, lightly straying
Over a sweet brow, idly playing
Had loosened from its braid such hair;
Since man from paradise was driven,
I swear the southern sun had never
Shone on a beauty half so fair.

8

She danced for the last time, in sorrow,
Alas! She knew that on the morrow
For her, Gudal's heir and his daughter,
Spirited child of liberty,
The sad fate of a slave girl beckoned,
A foreign land, as yet unreckoned,
And life in a strange family.
And her bright face was often shadowed
By clandestine uncertainty
And every movement, every gesture
Was so graceful, so expressive,
So full of sweet simplicity
That, had the Demon, flying over,
Upon her chanced to cast his eye,
Recalling then his former brothers
He would have turned away and sighed.

И Демон видел… На мгновенье
Неизъяснимое волненье
В себе почувствовал он вдруг.
Немой души его пустыню
Наполнил благодатный звук –
И вновь постигнул он святыню
Любви, добра и красоты!..
И долго сладостной картиной
Он любовался – и мечты
О прежнем счастье цепью длинной,
Как будто за звездой звезда,
Пред ним катилися тогда.
Прикованный незримой силой,
Он с новой грустью стал знаком;
В нем чувство вдруг заговорило
Родным когда-то языком.
То был ли признак возрожденья?
Он слов коварных искушенья
Найти в уме своем не мог…
Забыть? забвенья не дал бог:
Да он и не взял бы забвенья!..

9

The demon saw her... In a moment
An inexplicable emotion
Was stirred to life within his heart,
And his dumb soul, a boundless desert,
Resounded with a blessed note;
He once again received the sacred
Gift of beauty, warmth and love.
And for some time he watched that precious
Scene, and all the memories of
His former joy, in long succession,
Like star proceeding after star,
Passing before his eyes he saw.
By some unseen power fettered
He felt a pain he had not known.
Emotion's voice spoke up within him
As if it spoke in his own tongue.
Was it a sign of resurrection?
No words of treacherous seduction
Could he now find within his mind.
Forget? Oblivion God denied.
Besides, he did not want oblivion.

translated by Rose France

Гроб Оссиана

Под занавесою тумана,
Под небом бурь, среди степей,
Стоит могила Оссиана
В горах Шотландии моей.
Летит к ней дух мой усыпленный,
Родимым ветром подышать
И от могилы сей забвенной
Вторично жизнь свою занять!..

Ossian's Grave

In the Highlands of Scotland I love,
Storm clouds curve down on the dark fields and strands,
With icy grey mist closing in from above –
Here Ossian's grave still stands.
In dreams my heart races to be there,
To deeply breathe in its native air –
And from this long-forgotten shrine
Take its second life as mine.

translated by Alan Riach

Русская песня

1

Клоками белый снег валится,
Что ж дева красная боится
  С крыльца сойти,
  Воды снести?
Как поп, когда он гроб несет,
Так песнь метелица поет,
  Играет,
И у тесовых у ворот
Дворовый пес все цепь грызет
  И лает…

2

Но не собаки лай печальный,
Не вой метели погребальный
  Рождают страх
  В ее глазах;
Недавно милый схоронен,
Бледней снегов предстанет он
  И скажет:
«Ты изменила», – ей в лицо,
И ей заветное кольцо
  Покажет!..

Russian Song

1

The sky is full of snowflakes flying,
And on the step a girl stands, sighing,
Afraid to bring
The water in;
And like a priest a prayer intoning,
Sounds the blizzard's mournful moaning
And howling.
And all the while, beside the gate,
The dog is biting at his chain
And growling.

2

But not that growling, deep and low,
Nor yet the keening of the snow
Brightens her stare
With sudden fear;
Fresh in the grave her sweetheart lies,
Paler than snows he will arise
To go to her:
Then he will say: 'You played me false'
And the ring that plights their troth
He'll show her.

translated by Rose France

Желание

Зачем я не птица, не ворон степной,
  Пролетевший сейчас надо мной?
Зачем не могу в небесах я парить
  И одну лишь свободу любить?

На запад, на запад помчался бы я,
  Где цветут моих предков поля,
Где в замке пустом, на туманных горах,
  Их забвенный покоится прах.

На древней стене их наследственный щит
  И заржавленный меч их висит.
Я стал бы летать над мечом и щитом,
  И смахнул бы я пыль с них крылом;

И арфы шотландской струну бы задел,
  И по сводам бы звук полетел;
Внимаем одним и одним пробужден,
  Как раздался, так смолкнул бы он.

Но тщетны мечты, бесполезны мольбы
  Против строгих законов судьбы.
Меж мной и холмами отчизны моей
  Расстилаются волны морей,

Последний потомок отважных бойцов
  Увядает средь чуждых снегов;
Я здесь был рожден, но нездешний душой…
  О! зачем я не ворон степной?..

A Wish

Why am I not a bird – a raven?
How I'd soar, high into the heavens.
I'd love nothing more than to be free –
A black raven of the steppe I'd be.

Over the grassy seas, I'd fly west,
My shadow written on emptiness.
I'd come to the fields and stone towers,
Where once my forebears flowered.

In an old castle, shrouded in mist,
Their ashes lie in forgotten kists.
In the echoing vault of a great hall,
The ancestral shield hangs on a wall,

A rusty sword beside it. I'd brush
Away their long-held dust with a touch
Of my wing and I'd make the vaults ring
With the pluck of a Scottish harp's string.

But who else would be there to hear it
In the silence? Oh I more than fear it! –
That dreams are vain and prayers grate
Against the harsh stony court of fate.

The last of the brave warriors melts
Into alien snows; he too has felt
The weight of all the world's oceans,
Deepening between us.

I was born here, it's true! But I live
Far from here in my soul. Oh, I'd give
Everything that's precious up
To be a raven – a raven of the steppe.

translated by Tom Pow

* * *

Кто в утро зимнее, когда валит
Пушистый снег и красная заря
На степь седую с трепетом глядит,
Внимал колоколам монастыря;
В борьбе с порывным ветром этот звон
Далеко им по небу унесен, –
И путникам он нравился не раз,
Как весть кончины иль бессмертья глас.

И этот звон люблю я! Он цветок
Могильного кургана, мавзолей,
Который не изменится; ни рок,
Ни мелкие несчастия людей
Его не заглушат; всегда один,
Высокой башни мрачный властелин,
Он возвещает миру все, но сам –
Сам чужд всему, земле и небесам.

'If on a winter's morning'

If on a winter's morning, when the snow
Falls thick and soft, and the red dawn
Peers hesitantly at the hoary steppe,
You hear the bells ring in the monastery,
In battle with the blustering wind, the sound
Is carried by it far across the sky –
A sweet sound to the traveller on the road:
Death knell or voice of immortality.

I love that ringing! To me it is a flower
Upon a burial mound, a mausoleum
Unchanged by time. Not fate
Nor yet the petty trials of men
Shall have the power to stifle it. All alone,
The gloomy master of a lofty tower,
It speaks of all things to the world, and yet
Is lost to all things, lost to heaven and earth.

translated by Rose France

Ангел

По небу полуночи ангел летел,
  И тихую песню он пел;
И месяц, и звезды, и тучи толпой
  Внимали той песне святой.

Он пел о блаженстве безгрешных духов
  Под кущами райских садов;
О боге великом он пел, и хвала
  Его непритворна была.

Он душу младую в объятиях нес
  Для мира печали и слез;
И звук его песни в душе молодой
  Остался – без слов, но живой.

И долго на свете томилась она,
  Желанием чудным полна;
И звуков небес заменить не могли
  Ей скучные песни земли.

Angel

An angel flew through deep midnight
Softly singing a melody;
Clouds and moon and starry light
Received that sacred threnody.

The angel sang of blessed souls
Inhabiting the groves of heaven
And the mighty Lord of all
Praised in song unfeigning.

A young soul in the angel's arms
Intended for this realm of tears,
Enfolded in those wordless strains
Kept them within him through the years.

And through the weary days on earth
This strange yearning never failed
For all the songs of life and mirth
Could not usurp its wondrous hold.

translated by Tessa Ransford

* * *

Я не люблю тебя; страстей
И мук умчался прежний сон;
Но образ твой в душе моей
Все жив, хотя бессилен он;
Другим продавится мечтам,
Я все забыть его не мог;
Так храм оставленный – все храм,
Кумир поверженный – все бог!

'I don't love you'

I don't love you; the fevered dream
Of lust and longing's run its course.
Your image in my soul still seems
Alive, but it has lost its force.
I can't forget, hard though I worked
At other loves. It's not so odd:
The abandoned kirk is still a kirk,
The fallen idol – still a god!

translated by Peter McCarey

* * *

Нет, я не Байрон, я другой,
Еще неведомый избранник,
Как он, гонимый миром странник,
Но только с русскою душой.

Я раньше начал, кончу раньше,
Мой ум немного совершит;
В душе моей, как в океане,
Надежд разбитых груз лежит.

Кто может, океан угрюмый,
Твои изведать тайны? Кто
Толпе мои расскажет думы?
Я – или бог – или никто!

'Not Byron, but, like Byron'

Not Byron, but, like Byron, I
Am ostracised and ridiculed.
Russia is tattooed on my soul.
A chosen Byronobody,

I started sooner. I will die too soon.
Flood tides of genius drown my brain.
In my soul's ocean wrecked hulks moon,
Each smuggled hope a smithereen.

Dark Arctic Ocean, who can plumb
Your hidden deeps? No voice will call
Out of my deeps if I stay dumb.
I'm a god – or nobody at all!

translated by Robert Crawford

* * *

Она не гордой красотою
Прельщает юношей живых,
Она не водит за собою
Толпу вздыхателей немых.
И стан ее не стан богини,
И грудь волною не встает,
И в ней никто своей святыни,
Припав к земле, не признает.
Однако все ее движенья,
Улыбки, речи и черты
Так полны жизни, вдохновенья,
Так полны чудной простоты.
Но голос душу проникает,
Как воспоминанье лучших дней,
И сердце любит и страдает,
Почти стыдясь любви своей.

'She does not with disdainful beauty'

She does not with disdainful beauty
Seek to entice the lively young,
Nor does she lead, scornful and haughty,
Admirers in a sighing throng.
Nor is her figure truly divine,
Nor does her breast curve like a wave;
No one would fall to the ground, enshrine
Her in his heart, become her slave.
And yet and yet her every movement,
Feature, and utterance and smile
Are redolent of life, so brilliant,
Simple, and so free from guile.
While her voice pierces the spirit
Like a warm touch of days gone by;
And the heart loves yet suffers to hear it,
As though it might that love deny.

translated by Anna Crowe

Парус

Белеет парус одинокий
В тумане моря голубом!..
Что ищет он в стране далекой?
Что кинул он в краю родном?..

Играют волны – ветер свищет,
И мачта гнется и скрипит…
Увы, – он счастия не ищет
И не от счастия бежит!

Под ним струя светлей лазури,
Над ним луч солнца золотой…
А он, мятежный, просит бури,
Как будто в бурях есть покой!

Sail

A single sail a blaze of white
through haze on a pale blue sea!
What does it seek on a far-off shore?
What's left at the harbour quay?

Wind shrills, waves in a reel,
The masthead creaks and sways…
Alas, no course for happiness,
Nor flight from that, alas!

Below, a stream of sapphire light,
With sun's gold light on the helm…
Unruly, though, it invites the storm,
as if the storm brought calm!

translated by Alexander Hutchison

* * *

В рядах стояли безмолвной толпой,
  Когда хоронили мы друга;
Лишь поп полковой бормотал – и порой
  Ревела осенняя вьюга.
Кругом кивера над могилой святой
  Недвижны в тумане сверкали,
Уланская шапка да меч боевой
  На гробе дощатом лежали.
И билося сердце в груди не одно,
  И в землю все очи смотрели,
Как будто бы все, что уж ей отдано,
  Они у ней вырвать хотели.
Напрасные слезы из глаз не текли:
  Тоска наши души сжимала,
И горсть роковая прощальной земли,
  Упавши на гроб, застучала.
Прощай, наш товарищ, недолго ты жил,
  Певец с голубыми очами;
Лишь крест деревянный себе заслужил
  Да вечную память меж нами!

'Mute we stood'

Mute we stood, a silent army,
Formed to bury our friend.
Only the chaplain mumbled something,
Only the autumn blizzard blew –
While all around, over the sacred grave,
The shakos sparkled, still in the haze.
A lancer's hat and a battle-sword
Lay on the crude coffin,
And our hearts were hammers, pounding our chests,
And our eyes were drawn to the earth,
As if to claw back
All they'd given it.
No futile tears stained our faces,
Only the anguish crushed our souls
As a farewell fistful of clay
Clumped downwards, thudding the boards.
Goodbye, comrade, your span was short.
A blue-eyed bard you were –
And yet all you've won is a wooden cross
And our unforgetting.

translated by Christopher Rush and Anna Kurkina Rush

Еврейская мелодия
(Из Байрона)

Душа моя мрачна. Скорей, певец, скорей!
  Вот арфа золотая:
Пускай персты твои, промчавшися по ней,
  Пробудят в струнах звуки рая.
И если не навек надежды рок унес,
  Они в груди моей проснутся,
И если есть в очах застывших капля слез –
  Они растают и прольются.

Пусть будет песнь твоя дика. Как мои венец,
  Мне тягостны веселья звуки!
Я говорю тебе: я слез хочу, певец,
  Иль разорвется грудь от муки.
Страданьями была упитана она,
  Томилась долго и безмолвно;
И грозный час настал – теперь она полна,
  Как кубок смерти, яда полный.

Hebrew Melody
(from Byron)

My mood is dark. Quick, singer, hurry
Fetch your harp,
Strike the strings,
Release chords of peace.

Then if any hope in me survives
It may revive,
Then pent-up tears
Will melt and flow.

Make your song a wild one.
Cheerful sounds crush me like my crown.
Singer, give me tears, I say
Or my heart will crack.

My heart has fed on sorrow,
Too long kept silent.
Now the time of doom has come,
The cup of death is full.

translated by Tessa Ransford

Песня про царя Ивана Васильевича, молодого опричника и удалого купца Калашникова

Как на площади народ собирается,
Заунывный гудит-воет колокол,
Разглашает всюду весть недобрую.
По высокому месту лобному
Во рубахе красной с яркой запонкой,
С большим топором навостренныим,
Руки голые потираючи,
Палач весело похаживает,
Удалого бойца дожидается, –
А лихой боец, молодой купец,
Со родными братьями прощается:

«Уж вы, братцы мои, други кровные,
Поцелуемтесь да обнимемтесь
На последнее расставание.
Поклонитесь от меня Алене Дмитревне,
Закажите ей меньше печалиться,
Про меня моим детушкам не сказывать;
Поклонитесь дому родительскому,
Поклонитесь всем нашим товарищам,
Помолитесь сами в церкви божией
Вы за душу мою, душу грешную!»

И казнили Степана Калашникова
Смертью лютою, позорною;
И головушка бесталанная
Во крови на плаху покатилася.

Схоронили его за Москвой-рекой,
На чистом поле промеж трех дорог:
Промеж Тульской, Рязанской, Владимирской,
И бугор земли сырой тут насыпали,
И кленовый крест тут поставили.
И гуляют-шумят ветры буйные
Над его безымянной могилкою.

Song of the Tsar Ivan Vasilyevich, the Young Oprichnik Kiribeevich and the Brave Merchant Stepan Kalashnikov – Conclusion

… And the folk foregather on the square
As the bell dunnles dourly, across the land
Spreading news of foul acts.
Up on stage for the execution,
In his red sark with its shiny studs,
The headsman parades his fancy duds,
Carefully fondles his keen new axe;
Rubs his hands, in expectation
Of that brave fighter, the young merchant,
Ascending the wooden stair,
Taking leave of his brotherly band.

'Brothers – friends – my dear blood-brothers all,
This is our last, our loving last embrace,
Before we… part. We'll meet no more. Greet gently
My dearest wife, Alyona Dmitrevna;
Ask her not to give in to grieving,
Nor speak of me to the bairns;
Greet gently my parents' home,
Greet gently our comrades,
All of them; in church, I bid you pray
For my poor soul: my soul which lost its way.'

Cruelty and shame for Stepan
   The shudder and the shock,
As the doomed head of Stepan
   Rolled bloodily on the block.

They buried him by the Moscow river,
In that broad field of the three ways,
The roads to Tula, Ryazan, and Vladímir;
They built a tumulus of the moist earth,
And set a cross there, of the maple-wood.
The winds blatter and skelp, the storm will rave
Over this anonymous grave,

И проходят мимо люди добрые:
Пройдет стар человек – перекрестится,
Пройдет молодец – приосанится,
Пройдет девица – пригорюнится,
А пройдут гусляры – споют песенку.

*

Гей вы, ребята удалые,
Гусляры молодые,
Голоса заливные!
Красно начинали - красно и кончайте,
Каждому правдою и честью воздайте.
Тороватому боярину слава!
И красавице боярыне слава!
И всему народу христианскому слава!

And the good folk will come by:
An auld bodach comes by – he crosses himself;
A young lad comes by – fair cuts a dash –
A young lass comes by – she kneels in mourning,
The bards come by – they bring their songs.

★

Ach, you bonny brave fellas,
Young maestros of the *gusli*,
Give it laldie with your voices!
You started braw, and you'll end braw.
Sing your praise-poems to the deserving:
 To the big-hearted laird – *slava!*
 To his well-favoured lady – *slava!*
 To all good Christian folk – *slava!*

translated by Tom Hubbard

[*The song tells of the merchant Kalashnikov, who avenges an insult to his wife by killing a Guard (Oprichnik) of Ivan the Terrible; the Tsar reluctantly orders the merchant's execution.*]

Смерть поэта

Погиб Поэт! – невольник чести –
Пал, оклеветанный молвой,
С свинцом в груди и жаждой мести,
Поникнув гордой головой!..
Не вынесла душа Поэта
Позора мелочных обид,
Восстал он против мнений света
Один, как прежде… и убит!
Убит!.. к чему теперь рыданья,
Пустых похвал ненужный хор
И жалкий лепет оправданья?
Судьбы свершился приговор!
Не вы ль сперва так злобно гнали
Его свободный, смелый дар
И для потехи раздували
Чуть затаившийся пожар?
Что ж? веселитесь… он мучений
Последних вынести не мог:
Угас, как светоч, дивный гений,
Увял торжественный венок.

Его убийца хладнокровно
Навел удар… спасенья нет:
Пустое сердце бьется ровно,
В руке не дрогнул пистолет.
И что за диво?.. издалёка,
Подобный сотням беглецов,
На ловлю счастья и чинов
Заброшен к нам по воле рока;
Смеясь, он дерзко презирал
Земли чужой язык и нравы;
Не мог щадить он нашей славы;
Не мог понять в сей миг кровавый,
На что он руку поднимал!..

И он убит – и взят могилой,
Как тот певец, неведомый, но милый,

On the Death of a Poet

He's dead. Driven by his own honour
To death, ripped apart by lies and lead
And unquenched vengeance
And now he lowers his head.

He had a poet's soul and it was
Pierced by a thousand thin blades
Of malice. He took the bullies on
Alone and headstrong. And was slain.

He's dead. Stop your tears,
Your sobbed eulogies, beautiful tokens,
Excuses muttered under the breath –
Sentence is passed. The fates have spoken.

Wasn't it you who plagued him so,
Who stood on the hand that plucked the lyre
And blew the embers of rumour aflame
And fed the fire?

Well have your fill of laughing now
He's done for, he's dusty flesh –
The latest torments proved too much
His wreath is rosemary and ash.

His death was cold-blooded enough:
The hireling had a steady hand
A pistol with unswerving aim
And nothing where a heart might stand.

The henchman came from overseas
Like so many of his sort
To do his dirty business here
To find favour for it, and reward.

He laughed loudly and with contempt
Cared nothing for our ways, our tongue

Добыча ревности глухой,
Воспетый им с такою чудной силой,
Сраженный, как и он, безжалостной рукой.

Зачем от мирных нег и дружбы простодушной
Вступил он в этот свет завистливый и душный
Для сердца вольного и пламенных страстей?
Зачем он руку дал клеветникам ничтожным,
Зачем поверил он словам и ласкам ложным,
    Он, с юных лет постигнувший людей?..

И прежний сняв венок – они венец терновый,
Увитый лаврами, надели на него:
    Но иглы тайные сурово
    Язвили славное чело;
Отравлены его последние мгновенья
Коварным шепотом насмешливых невежд,
    И умер он – с напрасной жаждой мщенья,
С досадой тайною обманутых надежд.
    Замолкли звуки чудных песен,
    Не раздаваться им опять:
    Приют певца угрюм и тесен,
    И на устах его печать.

_____

    А вы, надменные потомки
Известной подлостью прославленных отцов,
Пятою рабскою поправшие обломки
Игрою счастия обиженных родов!
Вы, жадною толпой стоящие у трона,
Свободы, Гения и Славы палачи!
    Таитесь вы под сению закона,
    Пред вами суд и правда – все молчи!..
Но есть и божий суд, наперсники разврата!
    Есть грозный суд: он ждет;
    Он не доступен звону злата,
И мысли и дела он знает наперед.
Тогда напрасно вы прибегнете к злословью:

He cut down our brightest hope
And how could he begin to know
What he'd done?

Felled. Swallowed by the tomb
Like the other sweet boy who died unknown –
Driven on by his honour
Cut down by a murderer –
That boy the poet wrought in song.

But here's the mystery: he gave up his friends, his peace, for
that world
For those jackals with their stranglehold
On a free heart, on a passionate creature
He shook their hands,
He played their games –
He, who was the best judge of human nature!

They kicked off his laurel wreath
Put a crown of laurels and thorns on his head.
And the thorns tore his flesh
And his brow bled.
Even at the last, dragged through the mud
By mocking louts
He thirsted for revenge, and had none.
His hope ran out.

I want to hear his songs again:
They're fading out, the singer's done.
There's no singing from the grave.
It's dark and narrow where he's gone.

———————————————

But you're the children of Pharisees!
Slaves, who trample and grind
Men from unluckier families.
Butchers, crowding the throne hall,
Who answer genius and freedom with violence.

Оно вам не поможет вновь,
И вы не смоете всей вашей черной кровью
Поэта праведную кровь!

Hiding under the skirts of the law
And calling for truth to be gagged and silenced!
Haven't you heard of God's court, you scum?
He's waiting up there, scales and sword
And there's no crossing His palm
He knows what you did, and all you thought.

And all your gossiping, lying words were in vain
Now they will do you no more good!
Your black blood – all of it – won't wash out the stain
Of the poet's true blood.

translated by Sasha Dugdale

[In 1837 Russia's greatest poet, Aleksandr Pushkin, was shot dead in a duel
by the French soldier Georges d'Anthès, who had been pursuing his wife. The
'other sweet boy' is the poet Lensky, shot dead in a duel by the hero of Pushkin's
Eugene Onegin.]

Бородино

– Скажи-ка, дядя, ведь не даром
Москва, спаленная пожаром,
   Французу отдана?
Ведь были ж схватки боевые,
Да, говорят, еще какие!
Недаром помнит вся Россия
   Про день Бородина!

– Да, были люди в наше время,
Не то, что нынешнее племя:
   Богатыри – не вы!
Плохая им досталась доля:
Немногие вернулись с поля…
Не будь на то господня воля,
   Не отдали б Москвы!

Мы долго молча отступали,
Досадно было, боя ждали,
   Ворчали старики:
«Что ж мы? на зимние квартиры?
Не смеют, что ли, командиры
Чужие изорвать мундиры
   О русские штыки?»

И вот нашли большое поле:
Есть разгуляться где на воле!
   Построили редут.
У наших ушки на макушке!
Чуть утро осветило пушки
И леса синие верхушки –
   Французы тут как тут.

Borodino

'It wisna for nithin, wis it, Sarge,
That Moscow, sperkit, reduced to ash,
Wis handed ower t' Boney?
Surely oor boys were up for the schaw,
Aabody kens that they hud a richt go!
Aa Russia can gie ye blaw for blaw
On Borodino's story!'

'For sure, they swallt their tunics then,
Comparit to this lot they were men –
Titans – aye – nae feart.
Grim an coorse the fate that fell,
Just dribs and drabs at neist roll-call –
If it wisna for God-amichty's will,
Moscow wid still be there!

'We beat retreat for an age, lips ticht,
Scunnert an deeved, denied a fecht,
Aal squaddies girned – you bet!
"Are we stuck for winter up this spoot?
Will High Command nae gie's a hoot
T' rive the Frenchies' stuffin oot
Wi Sergei's bayonet?"

'An syne we fun a perk as lairge
As just micht suit oor heidlang chairge,
An biggit a gran redoot.
Noo aabody's lugs were richt oot flappin!
As Dawn pit licht t' ilka wappin,
The spruce trees shone bricht blue on tap –
An Boney on cue to come oot.

Забил заряд я в пушку туго
И думал: угощу я друга!
   Постой-ка, брат мусью!
Что тут хитрить, пожалуй к бою;
Уж мы пойдем ломить стеною,
Уж постоим мы головою
   За родину свою!

Два дня мы были в перестрелке.
Что толку в этакой безделке?
   Мы ждали третий день.
Повсюду стали слышны речи:
«Пора добраться до картечи!»
И вот на поле грозной сечи
   Ночная пала тень.

Прилег вздремнуть я у лафета,
И слышно было до рассвета,
   Как ликовал француз.
Но тих был наш бивак открытый:
Кто кивер чистил весь избитый,
Кто штык точил, ворча сердито,
   Кусая длинный ус.

И только небо засветилось,
Все шумно вдруг зашевелилось,
   Сверкнул за строем строй.
Полковник наш рожден был хватом;
Слуга царю, отец солдатам…
Да, жаль его: сражен булатом,
   Он спит в земле сырой.

И молвил он, сверкнув очами:
«Ребята! не Москва ль за нами?
   Умремте ж под Москвой,
Как наши братья умирали!»
И умереть мы обещали,
И клятву верности сдержали
   Мы в Бородинский бой.

'Richt doon the barrel I thumpit the shot.
"This ane's yours, pal!" 's fit I thocht.
"Heids up, Monsewer, Mon Frère!
Nae messin aboot, let's git tee it;
Brak oot like a michty waa t' dee it;
We'll ding oor nappers – nivver rue it –
For hamelan, aye, richt here!"

'For twa days lang we traded shells –
Nae muckle sense in yon, hell's bells!
Jist hingin for day three.
Near aabody thocht that cam in sicht,
The time for grape and shot wis richt.
The grun was bathed in shade o nicht
By bleed an crueltie.

'Doon next to ma gun I'd twa/three winks,
Richt throwe till dawn aal Boney's jinks
Cwid easily be heard.
Nae soun fae us, the bivvy still:
A mochie bearskin patched by Bill,
An Ivan grumphed as he stroppit ees steel
An chowed the strans o ees beard.

'As seen as the sky kythed a blink o licht
There wis plinty din steert up aaricht,
File glittered eftir file.
Oor colonel wis a staunch aal bird:
Leil t' the Tsar; a chiel t' his gairds –
Peety he's chappit by steel doon herd,
An sleeps aneth damp sile.

'He eggit us on, his een alicht:
"Boys, Moscow's ay ahint us, richt?
Lat's dee on the ootskirts noo!
Oor brithers wint doon afore us here,
They swore as we are bound to sweir;
In Borodino, nowt t' fear,
We'll keep oor solemn vow."

Ну ж был денек! Сквозь дым летучий
Французы двинулись, как тучи,
  И все на наш редут.
Уланы с пестрыми значками,
Драгуны с конскими хвостами,
Все промелькнули перед нами,
  Все побывали тут.

Вам не видать таких сражений!..
Носились знамена, как тени,
  В дыму огонь блестел,
Звучал булат, картечь визжала,
Рука бойцов колоть устала,
И ядрам пролетать мешала
  Гора кровавых тел.

Изведал враг в тот день немало,
Что значит русский бой удалый,
  Наш рукопашный бой!..
Земля тряслась – как наши груди;
Смешались в кучу кони, люди,
И залпы тысячи орудий
  Слились в протяжный вой…

Вот смерклось. Были все готовы
Заутра бой затеять новый
  И до конца стоять…
Вот затрещали барабаны –
И отступили бусурманы.
Тогда считать мы стали раны,
  Товарищей считать.

'Christ, fit a day! Throwe driftin smoke
The French cam on wi cloods for cloaks,
And heided richt oor wye.
The Lancers flashed across the grun,
Dragoons wi tassels pranced aroon;
This was far they aa were bound,
An far they socht to stey.

'You winna see sic as yon schaw noo –
The pennants wickerin fro an to,
In reek the flichter o fire.
The buckshot skraiched, syne clesh o steel,
Frae sinderin flesh your airm wid fail,
And cannonbaas jist sunk in the pile
That's deid – a bluiddy pyre.

'The enemy's gotten some lissons forby,
On fit it cost to grapple yon wye –
Wi Rooskies haun-t'-haun!
The yird – just lik oor herts – resiled,
Wi, horses, sodgers, strewn in a pile,
An thoosans o guns went aff wi a wail
An lingert abeen the land.

'Syne gloamin's there, an aa preparit,
Fan dawnin's bricht reveille blarit,
T' hud richt til the eyn.
An neisht the reeshle o drums was heard –
The 'ootlans' retrait, a wee bit yird,
An we took coont o wounds that fleert,
An talliet our stricken freens.

Да, были люди в наше время,
Могучее, лихое племя:
   Богатыри – не вы.
Плохая им досталась доля
Немногие вернулись с поля.
Когда б на то не божья воля,
   Не отдали б Москвы!

'Ach, they were men aroon yon time,
Bighairted, gallus, in their prime:
Aye, Titans, nae lik you!
Cruel dree wis theirs, an aince it fell,
Nae mony surfaced oot o yon bield.
Tho were it nae for God's ain will,
They'd bide far Moscow stood!'

translated by Alexander Hutchison

sperkit fired; *schaw* muster; *swallt* filled; *feart* scared; *coorse* bad; *neist* next; *scunnert* fed-up; *deeved* annoyed; *girned* groused; *rive* tear; *syne* then; *perk* field; *biggit* built; *ilka wappin* every weapon; *fit* what; *waa* wall; *ding* break; *nappers* heads; *hingin* waiting; *grun* ground; *cwid* could; *bivvy* bivouac; *mochie* tattered; *kythed* revealed; *steert* stirred; *chiel* chum; *chappit* chopped; *sile* soil; *far* where; *wickerin* waving; *reek* smoke; *flichter* glint; *sinderin* slicing; *forby* subsequently; *yird* earth; *resiled* shrank back; *fan* when; *hud* hold; *reeshle* rattle; *ootlans* foreigners; *talliet* counted; *gallus* spirited; *dree* fate; *bield* shelter

[The battle of Borodino (1812) was a particularly bloody encounter between Napoleon's invading Grande Armée and the Russian army. Though the Russians failed to prevent Napoleon marching on Moscow, the battle was a turning-point in the conflict.]

Сосед

Кто б ни был ты, печальный мой сосед,
Люблю тебя, как друга юных лет,
  Тебя, товарищ мой случайный,
Хотя судьбы коварною игрой
Навеки мы разлучены с тобой
  Стеной теперь – а после тайной.

Когда зари румяный полусвет
В окно тюрьмы прощальный свой привет
  Мне, умирая, посылает
И, опершись на звучное ружье,
Наш часовой, про старое житье
  Мечтая, стоя засыпает, –

Тогда, чело склонив к сырой стене,
Я слушаю – и в мрачной тишине
  Твои напевы раздаются.
О чем они – не знаю; но тоской
Исполнены, и звуки чередой,
  Как слезы, тихо льются, льются…

И лучших лет надежды и любовь –
В груди моей все оживает вновь,
  И мысли далеко несутся,
И полон ум желаний и страстей,
И кровь кипит – и слезы из очей,
  Как звуки, друг за другом льются.

Neighbour

Whoever you may be, my sad neighbour,
I love you like a friend of my young days,
    Love you, my accidental brother,
No matter how a wretched cast of fate
Forever keeps the two of us estranged,
    Now by a wall, and soon the secret.

Just as the first red gloaming light of dawn
Appearing at the prison window sends,
    Dying, its farewell greeting to me,
And on a crutch of his resounding gun
Our drowsy sentry, sleeping on his feet,
    Nods over, dreaming of the old life,

Then, forehead tilted to the damp stone wall,
I listen – and through the cheerless hush
    Your steady melodies sound freely.
Of what they speak, I don't know; yet my heart
Is charged with sorrow, and the measured tones,
    Like tears, softly, are flowing, flowing...

And better days of hope and love rise up,
Awakening again within my breast,
    And carry thought to distant places,
And longing and strong feeling seize my mind,
And my blood surges, and from my eyes tears
    Like your notes, flow, one after other.

translated by Colin Donati

* * *

Когда волнуется желтеющая нива,
И свежий лес шумит при звуке ветерка,
И прячется в саду малиновая слива
Под тенью сладостной зеленого листка;

Когда, росой обрызганный душистой,
Румяным вечером иль утра в час златой,
Из-под куста мне ландыш серебристый
Приветливо кивает головой;

Когда студеный ключ играет по оврагу
И, погружая мысль в какой-то смутный сон,
Лепечет мне таинственную сагу
Про мирный край, откуда мчится он, –

Тогда смиряется души моей тревога,
Тогда расходятся морщины на челе, –
И счастье я могу постигнуть на земле,
И в небесах я вижу бога.

'Whan the yallowin cornfield's fair steirin'

Whan the yallowin cornfield's fair steirin,
And the cuil wuid's reeslin i the souch,
And the gairden's cramasie fruit is beeryin
Itsel neth thon hinnie-sweet leafy neuk;

Whan wi the scentit dew hit's skimmerin,
At gloamin-time or dawin-oor,
Frae unner a buss, the lilikin
Boos its wee heid: a frienly flouer;

Whan the cauldrife burn doun the glen is spielin
Slungin my thochts ti a dootsome dwam,
Slabberin ti me an unco Hielan
Tale, as it breenges frae lands o calm;

Than, my lang wanrest nae mair is deavin
My hert, the runkles on my brou
Are smuithed, and in the here-and-nou
I'm blythe, and I see God in Heiven.

translated by Tom Hubbard

yallowin yellowing; *steirin* stirring; *reeslin* rustling; *souch* breeze; *cramasie* crimson; *beeryin* burying; *neth* beneath; *thon* that; *hinnie-sweet* honey-sweet; *neuk* corner; *skimmerin* twinkling; *dawin-oor* dawn; *buss* bush; *lilikin* lily-of-the-valley; *boos* bows; *cauldrife* cold; *spielin* playing; *slungin* plunging; *dootsome* uncertain; *dwam* trance; *slabberin* babbling; *unco* uncanny; *breenges* rushes forward; *wanrest* anxiety; *deavin* troubling

* * *

Расстались мы, но твой портрет
Я на груди моей храню:
Как бледный призрак лучших лет,
Он душу радует мою.

И, новым преданный страстям,
Я разлюбить его не мог:
Так храм оставленный – все храм,
Кумир поверженный – все бог!

'We parted'

We parted, but your portrait still
Is in its locket, at my breast –
A watermark from joy that filled
Me in the years I loved the best.
Though new affairs have made their mark
It won't be ousted or outlawed;
The abandoned kirk is still a kirk,
The fallen idol – still a god!

translated by Peter McCarey

Кинжал

Люблю тебя, булатный мой кинжал,
Товарищ светлый и холодный.
Задумчивый грузин на месть тебя ковал,
На грозный бой точил черкес свободный.

Лилейная рука тебя мне поднесла
В знак памяти, в минуту расставанья,
И в первый раз не кровь вдоль по тебе текла,
Но светлая слеза – жемчужина страданья.

И черные глаза, остановясь на мне,
Исполненны таинственной печали,
Как сталь твоя при трепетном огне,
То вдруг тускнели, то сверкали.

Ты дан мне в спутники, любви залог немой,
И страннику в тебе пример не бесполезный:
Да, я не изменюсь и буду тверд душой,
Как ты, как ты, мой друг железный.

The Dagger

Ah lo'e ye ma steel dagger Damascene,
Ma leal an trusty fiere that's bricht an cauld,
An ill-daein Georgian forgit ye fir saut,
A free Circassian straik ye fir the fecht.

A lily white haund haes brochten ye tae me,
A mindin o the moment o oor pairtin,
Nae bluid rin doun ye at yer kirstenin,
But ae bricht tear, a pearl o sufferin.

An thae daurk een that cam tae rest oan me,
Wir lippin-fou o dowf uncanniness,
Jist lik your steel held in the dwaiblie flame,
Nou suddentlike growes dim, nou brichtly glents.

Thou seelent fiere, gien as a pledge o luve,
There's lear in you ah'll mind throu ma stravaigin,
Aye, ah'll nae chynge, ah'm siccar in ma saul,
Lik ye, lik ye, ma unbowsome iron frien.

translated by Rab Wilson

leal loyal; *fiere* friend, comrade; *ill-daein* badly behaved; *saut* literally salt, but here means revenge; *straik* honed, sharpened; *mindin* reminder; *kirstenin* christening; *lippin-fou* brimming over; *dowf* sad, weary; *dwaiblie* wavering, feeble; *glents* gleams; *seelent* silent; *lear* learning, wisdom; *stravaigin* wandering, travels; *chynge* change; *siccar* secure; *unbowsome* unyielding

* * *

Гляжу на будущность с боязнью,
Гляжу на прошлое с тоской
И, как преступник перед казнью,
Ищу кругом души родной;
Придет ли вестник избавленья
Открыть мне жизни назначенье,
Цель упований и страстей,
Поведать – что мне бог готовил,
Зачем так горько прекословил
Надеждам юности моей.

Земле я отдал дань земную
Любви, надежд, добра и зла;
Начать готов я жизнь другую,
Молчу и жду: пора пришла;
Я в мире не оставлю брата,
И тьмой и холодом объята
Душа усталая моя;
Как ранний плод, лишенный сока,
Она увяла в бурях рока
Под знойным солнцем бытия.

'I backward cast my e'e'

I backward cast my e'e
On prospects drear!
An' forward tho' I canna see
I guess and fear!

And like a criminal before execution,
I search for a kindred spirit,
a truth-teller to set me free,
by laying before me life's purpose;
the point of both expectation
and passion, to reveal what God's plan
for me might be – and why he has
so cruelly reversed the dreams
of my youth. The earth now holds
my earthly debts – the loves and hopes
that once I cherished; both the good
and the evil that I have done.

The time has come for a different
kind of life, now I am brotherless
on earth. I wait in silence
for this new life to begin.
    But my tired soul
is cold, wrapped up in darkness.
Like a young fruit, it has withered
in the storm and unforgiving sun.

translated by Tom Pow

[The first four lines are from Burns's 'To a Mouse'; they seem to be echoed in Lermontov's poem.]

* * *

Она поет – и звуки тают,
Как поцелуи на устах,
Глядит – и небеса играют
В ее божественных глазах;

Идет ли – все ее движенья,
Иль молвит слово – все черты
Так полны чувства, выраженья,
Так полны дивной простоты.

'She sings'

She sings. The songs quiver
Like kissed flames.
She glances, a giver
Of constellations,

Her catwalk clarity
Vivid, when she speaks,
With a dancer's harmony,
An arrow of articulation.

translated by Robert Crawford

Казачья колыбельная песня

Спи, младенец мой прекрасный,
  Баюшки-баю.
Тихо смотрит месяц ясный
  В колыбель твою.
Стану сказывать я сказки,
  Песенку спою;
Ты ж дремли, закрывши глазки,
  Баюшки-баю.

По камням струится Терек,
  Плещет мутный вал;
Злой чечен ползет на берег,
  Точит свой кинжал;
Но отец твой старый воин,
  Закален в бою:
Спи, малютка, будь спокоен,
  Баюшки-баю.

Сам узнаешь, будет время,
  Бранное житье;
Смело вденешь ногу в стремя
  И возьмешь ружье.
Я седельце боевое
  Шелком разошью…
Спи, дитя мое родное,
  Баюшки-баю.

Богатырь ты будешь с виду
  И казак душой.
Провожать тебя я выйду я
  Ты махнешь рукой…
Сколько горьких слез украдкой
  Я в ту ночь пролью!..
Спи, мой ангел, тихо, сладко,
  Баюшки-баю.

Cossack Cradle Song

Sleep, my baby, sleep, my beauty,
    Bayushki-bayu.
Bright the quiet moon is shining,
    Shining over you.
I will sit and tell you stories,
    Sing a song for you;
Close your little eyes and slumber,
    Bayushki-bayu.

Terek ripples over pebbles,
    Splashing with dark life;
Fierce the Chechen steals across it
    With his wicked knife;
But your father's an old warrior
    Hardened in the fight;
Sleep, my baby, never worry,
    Gently lullaby.

You will see, the day is coming –
    In the ranks you'll stand;
Bravely leap up on the stirrups,
    A rifle in your hand.
And I'll decorate your saddle,
    Silken threads I'll sew…
Sleep, my own, my darling baby,
    Bayushki-bayu.

You will be a mighty champion,
    A cossack true and brave.
As you go riding from the village,
    You'll greet me with a wave…
But I'll weep, tears oh so bitter,
    All the wakeful night!…
Sleep, my angel, sleep so sweetly,
    Gently lullaby.

Стану я тоской томиться,
  Безутешно ждать;
Стану целый день молиться,
  По ночам гадать;
Стану думать, что скучаешь
  Ты в чужом краю…
Спи ж, пока забот не знаешь,
  Баюшки-баю.

Дам тебе я на дорогу
  Образок святой:
Ты его, моляся богу,
  Ставь перед собой;
Да готовясь в бой опасный,
  Помни мать свою…
Спи, младенец мой прекрасный,
  Баюшки-баю.

I'll be waiting for you, grieving,
    Ceaselessly I'll wait;
I'll be praying still and reading
    Fortunes every night;
I'll be thinking of you pining
    On a distant shore…
Sleep now, while you still are carefree,
    Bayushki-bayu.

I'll give you a holy image
    When you take the road:
don't forget to keep it by you
    When you pray to God.
When you're riding into danger,
    Still remember me…
Sleep, my baby, sleep my lovely,
    Gently lullaby.

translated by Peter France

Не верь себе

Не верь, не верь себе, мечтатель молодой,
    Как язвы, бойся вдохновенья…
Оно – тяжелый бред души твоей больной
    Иль пленной мысли раздраженье.
В нем признака небес напрасно не ищи:
    То кровь кипит, то сил избыток!
Скорее жизнь свою в заботах истощи,
    Разлей отравленный напиток!

Случится ли тебе в заветный, чудный миг
    Отрыть в душе давно безмолвной
Еще неведомый и девственный родник,
    Простых и сладких звуков полный, –
Не вслушивайся в них, не предавайся им,
    Набрось на них покров забвенья:
Стихом размеренным и словом ледяным
    Не передашь ты их значенья.

Закрадется ль печаль в тайник души твоей,
    Зайдет ли страсть с грозой и вьюгой, –
Не выходи тогда на шумный пир людей
    С своею бешеной подругой;
Не унижай себя. Стыдися торговать
    То гневом, то тоской послушной,
И гной душевных ран надменно выставлять
    На диво черни простодушной,

Какое дело нам, страдал ты или нет?
    На что нам знать твои волненья,
Надежды глупые первоначальных лет,
    Рассудка злые сожаленья?
Взгляни: перед тобой играючи идет
    Толпа дорогою привычной;
На лицах праздничных чуть виден след забот,
    Слезы не встретишь неприличной.

Never Trust Yourself

Young dreamer, never trust yourself,
Shun inspiration like the plague…
It is the sick soul's malady,
The chafing of a mind in chains.
Don't look to it for heavenly signs;
It's just hot blood, just youthful fire.
Better wear out your life with cares
And pour away the poisoned wine.

If in a precious moment you
Discover in your shuttered soul
An unseen, untouched spring that's full
Of simple sweetly-sounding notes,
Don't listen to them, stay aloof,
Bury them in oblivion;
Don't hope with metre and cold words
To pass their hidden meaning on.

Should sorrow creep into your soul
Or passion sound her cold alarm,
Don't show yourself among the crowd
With those mad playmates on your arm.
Be proud. Don't stoop to buy and sell
Your anger or your humble woes,
Nor let the stupid rabble tell
The tragic story of your wounds.

If you have suffered, do we care?
And do we need to know your heart,
The silly hopes of childish days
Or reason's torturing regret?
See how the crowd stroll playfully
Along their usual road; no cares
Disfigure their gay festivity,
They do not shed unseemly tears.

А между тем из них едва ли есть один,
   Тяжелой пыткой не измятый,
До преждевременных добравшийся морщин
   Без преступленья иль утраты!..
Поверь: для них смешон твой плач и твой укор,
   С своим напевом заученным,
Как разрумяненный трагический актер,
   Махающий мечом картонным…

Even so, scarcely one of them
Has never suffered from the lash,
Or reached untouched by loss or crime
The age where wrinkles plough the face!...
Believe me, your protesting cries
And sad refrains just seem absurd
To them – an actor daubed in grease
Waving a papier-maché sword...

translated by Peter France

Памяти А. И. Одевского

1

Я знал его: мы странствовали с ним
В горах востока, и тоску изгнанья
Делили дружно; но к полям родным
Вернулся я, и время испытанья
Промчалося законной чередой;
А он не дождался минуты сладкой:
Под бедною походною палаткой
Болезнь его сразила, и с собой
В могилу он унес летучий рой
Еще незрелых, темных вдохновений,
Обманутых надежд и горьких сожалений!

2

Он был рожден для них, для тех надежд,
Поэзии и счастья… Но, безумный –
Из детских рано вырвался одежд
И сердце бросил в море жизни шумной,
И свет не пощадил – и бог не спас!
Но до конца среди волнений трудных,
В толпе людской и средь пустынь безлюдных
В нем тихий пламень чувства не угас:
Он сохранил и блеск лазурных глаз,
И звонкий детский смех, и речь живую,
И веру гордую в людей и жизнь иную.

In Memory of A.I. Odoevsky

1

I knew him well, for he and I had wandered
Among the eastern hills; as friends we shared
The exile's melancholy; but I homeward
Turned at last, and weeks and months of hard-
ship hurried by, and I had served my time.
He, alas, did not live to see that moment:
Beneath the canvas of an army tent
Sickness struck him down; he died, and with him
To the grave he took a buzzing swarm
Of still half-formed, obscure and lofty plans,
Of hopes betrayed, and bitter turbulence.

2

It seemed that he was born for hopes like those
Of poetry and joy but, stubbornly,
He tore himself free of childish clothes
And threw his heart into life's noisy sea.
The world would not save him, nor did God raise
A finger. Yet, till the end, through all that strife,
In teeming crowds, or deserts void of life,
The quiet flame of feeling always blazed;
And his eyes sparkled, blue as summer days,
His ringing, childish laugh, his voice's rhythms,
His proud belief in people and in heaven.

3

Но он погиб далеко от друзей…
Мир сердцу твоему, мой милый Саша!
Покрытое землей чужих полей,
Пусть тихо спит оно, как дружба наша
В немом кладбище памяти моей!
Ты умер, как и многие, без шума,
Но с твердостью. Таинственная дума
Еще блуждала на челе твоем,
Когда глаза закрылись вечным сном;
И то, что ты сказал перед кончиной,
Из слушавших тебя не понял ни единый…

4

И было ль то привет стране родной,
Названье ли оставленного друга,
Или тоска по жизни молодой,
Иль просто крик последнего недуга,
Кто скажет нам?.. Твоих последних слов
Глубокое и горькое значенье
Потеряно… Дела твои, и мненья,
И думы – все исчезло без следов,
Как легкий пар вечерних облаков:
Едва блеснут, их ветер вновь уносит –
Куда они? зачем? откуда? – кто их спросит…

3

And yet he perished far from all his friends…
Peace, my dear Sasha, to your faithful heart
That's covered by the soil of foreign lands!
May it sleep, like our friendship, still and quiet
In my remembrance's silent graveyard.
You died, as many die – no noise, no fuss –
But with resolve. And thought, mysterious,
Was lingering still upon your forehead.
Your eyes were closed, and you slept with the dead,
And what it was you said before the end
None of us listening there could comprehend.

4

For whether a greeting to your native heath,
Or name of friend whom you had left behind,
Or cry of grief and sorrow at lost youth,
Or affliction's grip upon you at the end,
Who now can tell us! Of your final words
The fierce, bitter and profound import
Is lost to us… Your actions and your thoughts,
Your meditations, all are flown like birds:
Like the light vapour made by evening clouds,
They scarcely shine before the wind harries them;
Where are they going, and why? From whence? Who
    questions them?

5

И после их на небе нет следа,
Как от любви ребенка безнадежной,
Как от мечты, которой никогда
Он не вверял заботам дружбы нежной…
Что за нужда?.. Пускай забудет свет
Столь чуждое ему существованье:
Зачем тебе венцы его вниманья
И терния пустых его клевет?
Ты не служил ему. Ты с юных лет
Коварные его отвергнул цепи:
Любил ты моря шум, молчанье синей степи –

6

И мрачных гор зубчатые хребты…
И вкруг твоей могилы неизвестной
Все, чем при жизни радовался ты,
Судьба соединила так чудесно:
Немая степь синеет, и венцом
Серебряным Кавказ ее объемлет;
Над морем он, нахмурясь, тихо дремлет,
Как великан склонившись над щитом,
Рассказам волн кочуюших внимая,
А море Черное шумит не умолкая.

5

And after, the sky is empty and they are lost,
Akin to childish love that's without hope
Or like a dream he never could entrust
Into the charge of tender-hearted friendship:
Where's the need? Let the world's oblivion
Fall on a spirit that it held as alien:
Why do you need its wreath of admiration
Or the crown of thorns its slanders pressed on you?
You never served it. When we were young, we two,
We held its treacherous claims in deep contempt.
You loved the wild sea, the blue and silent steppe –

6

And the toothed summits of the frowning mountains…
Around your unmarked grave on every side
Fate has miraculously brought together
All that so gladdened you before you died:
The silent steppe lies blue, and like a crown
The Caucasus embraces it with silver;
Above the sea it frowns in quiet slumber –
A giant over his shield bending down –
Hearing the wandering waves' long litanies,
That boom on Black Sea shores and never cease.

translated by Anna Crowe

* * *

Есть речи – значенье
Темно иль ничтожно,
Но им без волненья
Внимать невозможно.

Как полны их звуки
Безумством желанья!
В них слезы разлуки,
В них трепет свиданья,

Не встретит ответа
Средь шума мирского
Из пламя и света
Рожденное слово;

Но в храме, средь боя
И где я ни буду,
Услышав, его я
Узнаю повсюду.

Не кончив молитвы,
На звук тот отвечу,
И брошусь из битвы
Ему я навстречу.

'Words may be spoken'

Words may be spoken
Commonplace or obscure,
Yet we cannot hear them
Without being deeply stirred.

How their tones express
The frenzy of desire
Misery of separation
And ecstasy of union.

No answer can be found
Amid daily conversation
To such words as arise
Out of flame and light.

Whether in church or battle
Wherever I may be
When I hear the message
I know it straightaway.

I'll cut short my praying
To answer that call
And flee from the fray
Towards it, to hear it.

translated by Tessa Ransford

* * *

Как часто, пестрою толпою окружен,
Когда передо мной, как будто бы сквозь сон,
   При шуме музыки и пляски,
При диком шепоте затверженных речей,
Мелькают образы бездушные людей,
   Приличьем стянутые маски,

Когда касаются холодных рук моих
С небрежной смелостью красавиц городских
   Давно бестрепетные руки, –
Наружно погружась в их блеск и суету,
Ласкаю я в душе старинную мечту,
   Погибших лет святые звуки.

И если как-нибудь на миг удастся мне
Забыться, – памятью к недавней старине
   Лечу я вольной, вольной птицей;
И вижу я себя ребенком, и кругом
Родные всё места: высокий барский дом
   И сад с разрушенной теплицей;

Зеленой сетью трав подернут спящий пруд,
А за прудом село дымится – и встают
   Вдали туманы над полями.
В аллею темную вхожу я; сквозь кусты
Глядит вечерний луч, и желтые листы
   Шумят под робкими шагами.

И странная тоска теснит уж грудь мою:
Я думаю об ней, я плачу и люблю,
   Люблю мечты моей созданье
С глазами, полными лазурного огня,
С улыбкой розовой, как молодого дня
   За рощей первое сиянье.

'How often, as I stand in the bright crowd'

1st January

How often, as I stand in the bright crowd,
Where like a dream performed against the loud
   Cacophony of dancing music,
The hissing, whispered speeches learnt by heart,
Before my eyes the soulless figures float
   Cased in the masks of proper fashion,

And as I feel on my cold hands the touch,
The brazen hands of city beauties who
   Have learnt the art of never blushing,
While seeming to admire their hectic gleam,
I dwell in secret on an ancient dream,
   Its sacred sounds now half-forgotten.

And if somehow I find a way to flee
The world around me, like a bird set free
   I fly in memory to days now vanished;
I am again a child and all around
See places that I knew, the lofty house,
   The ruined greenhouse in the garden,

The sleeping pond caught in a net of weeds,
And then the village chimneys, and far off
   The mist that drifts over the clearings.
I enter the dark alley, where the light
Of evening threads the bushes, and my feet
   Tread shyly on the dun leaves' crackle.

Then a mysterious longing fills my heart,
I think of her and weep for her, I love,
   I love the one my dreams created,
Her eyes that sparkle with an azure fire,
Her smile as rosy as the dawning light
   Of day that breaks beyond the spinney.

Так царства дивного всесильный господин –
Я долгие часы просиживал один,
    И память их жива поныне
Под бурей тягостных сомнений и страстей,
Как свежий островок безвредно средь морей
    Цветет на влажной их пустыне.

Когда ж, опомнившись, обман я узнаю
И шум толпы людской спугнет мечту мою,
    На праздник незваную гостью,
О, как мне хочется смутить веселость их
И дерзко бросить им в глаза железный стих,
    Облитый горечью и злостью!..

There I would sit alone for hours on end,
All-powerful king of an enchanted land,
   And memory preserves that vision
Amidst the storms of passion and unease,
An isle of freshness in the brackish seas,
   Still blooming on the desolate water.

But when, awoken from that sleep, I see
My error and the crowds that shun my dream,
   As at a party they would shun a stranger,
Oh, how I want to spoil their merry games
By flinging in their face metallic lines
   Burnished by bitterness and anger!...

translated by Peter France

* * *

И скучно и грустно, и некому руку подать
     В минуту душевной невзгоды…
Желанья!.. что пользы напрасно и вечно желать?..
     А годы проходят – все лучшие годы!

Любить… но кого же?.. на время – не стоит труда,
     А вечно любить невозможно.
В себя ли заглянешь? – там прошлого нет и следа:
     И радость, и муки, и все там ничтожно…

Что страсти? – ведь рано иль поздно их сладкий недуг
     Исчезнет при слове рассудка;
И жизнь, как посмотришь с холодным вниманьем вокруг, –
     Такая пустая и глупая шутка…

'It's dull and it's sad'

It's dull and it's sad, and there's no-one to greet as a friend,
When your soul is beset by misfortune...
Desire? But why bother desiring without hope or end?
And the years hurry by, – all the best years are passing!

To love... but who is there? For a while it is not worth the pain,
And where can you find love eternal?
Or look into your heart? – Not a trace of the past there remains
And the joy, and the torments, they all seem quite futile.

And passion? That sweet-tasting sickness, you'll find
Disappears at the first touch of reason,
And life, when you take a cold, clear look around,
Is just a ridiculous joke, out of season.

translated by Rose France and Peter France

Журналист, читатель и писатель

Комната писателя; опущенные шторы. Он сидит в больших креслах перед камином. Читатель, с сигарой, стоит спиной к камину. Журналист входит.

Журналист

Я очень рад, что вы больны:
В заботах жизни, в шуме света
Теряет скоро ум поэта
Свои божественные сны.
Среди различных впечатлений
На мелочь душу разменяв,
Он гибнет жертвой общих мнений.
Когда ему в пылу забав
Обдумать зрелое творенье?..
Зато какая благодать,
Коль небо вздумает послать
Ему изгнанье, заточенье
Иль даже долгую болезнь:
Тотчас в его уединенье
Раздастся сладостная песнь!
Порой влюбляется он страстно
В свою нарядную печаль…
Ну, что вы пишете? нельзя ль
Узнать?

Писатель
Да ничего…

Журналист
        Напрасно!

Писатель
О чем писать? Восток и юг
Давно описаны, воспеты;
Толпу ругали все поэты,
Хвалили все семейный круг;
Все в небеса неслись душою,

Journalist, Reader and Writer

A writer's room. The blinds are lowered. He is sitting in a big armchair by the fire. A reader is standing with his back to the fire, smoking a cigar. A journalist comes in.

Journalist
I'm very glad to find you ill.
In the world's busy hurly-burly
The poet loses all too quickly
The god-like dreams that filled his soul.
Among the medley of impressions
Trading his spirit for small change,
He's soon in hock to common notions.
When has he time, when fun's the rage,
For some well-pondered composition?...
But what a blessing when kind fate
Thinks to bestow on him the gift
Of exile or incarceration
Or even long drawn-out disease:
For then he hears in isolation
A song, melodious and sweet!
It may be he will fall in love
With his enchanting melancholy...
So what are you writing? Can't you give
Me an idea?

   Writer
        Oh, nothing...

   Journalist
                        Really!

   Writer
What can we write about? The South
And East have long ago been painted;
Poets have all abused the crowd
And sung hymns to domestic virtue;
All have aspired to heaven and breathed

Взывали, с тайною мольбою,
К N. N., неведомой красе, –
И страшно надоели все,

Читатель
И я скажу – нужна отвага,
Чтобы открыть… хоть ваш журнал
(Он мне уж руки обломал):
Во-первых, серая бумага,
Она, быть может, и чиста,
Да как-то страшно без перчаток…
Читаешь – сотни опечаток!
Стихи – такая пустота;
Слова без смысла, чувства нету,
Натянут каждый оборот;
Притом – сказать ли по секрету?
И в рифмах часто недочет.
Возьмешь ли прозу? – перевод.
А если вам и попадутся
Рассказы на родимый лад -
То, верно, над Москвой смеются
Иди чиновников бранят.
С кого они портреты пишут?
Где разговоры эти слышут?
А если и случалось им,
Так мы их слышать не хотим…
Когда же на Руси бесплодной,
Расставшись с ложной мишурой,
Мысль обретет язык простой
И страсти голос благородный?

Журналист
Я точно то же говорю.
Как вы, открыто негодуя,
На музу русскую смотрю я,
Прочтите критику мою,

Читатель
Читал я. Мелкие нападки

A secret prayer to that rare beauty,
Miss X – and meanwhile everybody
That hears them has been bored to death.

Reader

I'll tell you – it demands some courage
To open… well, your magazine
(It sprains my wrist to pick it up):
Quite possibly the paper's clean,
But what a dismal greyish colour!…
You'd shrink to touch it without gloves…
And in the text, hundreds of misprints!
The poetry is feeble stuff;
No feeling, words without a meaning,
And sentences tied up in knots;
What's more – I'll say it in a whisper –
The rhymes are often not so hot.
As for the prose, it's all translation.
Or if you chance to hit upon
A story told in native Russian,
It's bound to be some witty satire
Of Moscow or the bureaucrats.
Where do they find these sitting ducks?
Where do they hear these conversations?
And even if they've chanced to hear them,
We've no desire to share the joke…
When shall we see in barren Russia
Minds that reject this empty noise
For simple language and a voice
That speaks with dignity of passion?

Journalist

I think the same as you, exactly.
Like you I make no secret of
My indignation at our poets.
Just read my articles.

Reader
                I have.

На шрифт, виньетки, опечатки,
Намеки тонкие на то,
Чего не ведает никто.
Хотя б забавно было свету!..
В чернилах ваших, господа,
И желчи едкой даже нету –
А просто грязная вода.

Журналист
И с этим надо согласиться.
Но верьте мне, душевно рад
Я был бы вовсе не браниться –
Да как же быть?.. меня бранят!
Войдите в наше положенье!
Читает нас и низший круг:
Нагая резкость выраженья
Не всякий оскорбляет слух;
Приличье, вкус – все так условно;
А деньги все ведь платят ровно!
Поверьте мне: судьбою несть
Даны нам тяжкие вериги.
Скажите, каково прочесть
Весь этот вздор, все эти книги, –
И все зачем? – чтоб вам сказать,
Что их не надобно читать!..

Читатель
Зато какое наслажденье,
Как отдыхает ум и грудь,
Коль попадется как-нибудь
Живое, свежее творенье!
Вот, например, приятель мой:
Владеет он изрядным слогом,
И чувств и мыслей полнотой
Он одарен всевышним богом.

Журналист
Все это так, да вот беда:
Не пишут эти господа.

I find they're full of petty quibbles
At typeface, misprints and vignettes,
Or subtle digs about some troubles
That no-one really knows about.
If only they were entertaining!…
My friends, your inkpots, truth to tell,
Contain no venom, nothing scathing,
But dirty water, nothing else.

Journalist

That's very true, I must admit it.
Believe me, I'd be very glad
To speak a language less insulting,
But they heap insults on my head!
Just put yourself in my position:
Even the lowest ranks can read,
And the most vulgar crude expression
Doesn't seem shocking to all ears.
Good taste and decent manners vary,
And anyway we get the money!
Believe me: we're condemned by fate
To ply our trade in heavy shackles.
Think what a pain it is to read
So many books and so much twaddle, –
And to what end? so we can say:
'You need not read this book today.'

Reader

But then what a delight it is,
How mind and soul sigh with relief,
When by some chance they get a vision
Of a fresh, lively, new creation!
For instance, take this friend of mine:
He has a pretty decent style,
And the gods have bestowed upon him
Feelings and thoughts in rich abundance.

Journalist

All very well, but here's the rub:
Such gentlemen don't write a word.

Писатель

О чем писать?.. Бывает время,
Когда забот спадает бремя,
Дни вдохновенного труда,
Когда и ум и сердце полны,
И рифмы дружные, как волны,
Журча, одна вослед другой
Несутся вольной чередой.
Восходит чудное светило
В душе проснувшейся едва:
На мысли, дышащие силой,
Как жемчуг нижутся слова...
Тогда с отвагою свободной
Поэт на будущность глядит,
И мир мечтою благородной
Пред ним очищен и обмыт.
Но эти странные творенья
Читает дома он один,
И ими после без зазренья
Он затопляет свой камин.
Ужель ребяческие чувства,
Воздушный, безотчетный бред
Достойны строгого искусства?
Их осмеет, забудет свет...

Бывают тягостные ночи:
Без сна, горят и плачут очи,
На сердце – жадная тоска;
Дрожа, холодная рука
Подушку жаркую объемлет;
Невольный страх власы подъемлет;
Болезненный, безумный крик
Из груди рвется – и язык
Лепечет громко без сознанья
Давно забытые названья;
Давно забытые черты
В сиянье прежней красоты
Рисует память своевольно:
В очах любовь, в устах обман –
И веришь снова им невольно,

Writer

What can we write? There are occasions
When we can shake off worry's burden,
And inspiration fills our days;
The mind and heart are full to bursting,
And rhymes companionable as waves
Come running, babbling as they go,
In an unfettered endless flow.
A star miraculously rises
Within the still half-sleeping soul,
And words like pearls thread themselves nicely
On thoughts that seem infused with power…
At times like this a poet gazes
With a bold heart on future times,
And the whole world is spread before him
All washed and clean, a noble dream.
But these peculiar creations
He only reads at home, alone,
And then without a twinge of conscience
He feeds the papers to his stove.
Can he believe these childish feelings,
These airy, unencumbered dreams,
Are worthy of the artist's calling?
Men will forget them, laugh at them…

And then there are oppressive nights
With sleepless, burning, weeping eyes
And a heart filled with hungry longing;
Your hand, bitterly cold and trembling,
Clings to an overheated pillow;
Involuntarily, in fear
Your hair stands up; a sick mad bellow
Bursts from your breast, and loud and clear,
Your tongue unconsciously repeats
Names that have long since been forgotten;
And memory capriciously
Exhumes long since forgotten features,
The splendour of their former beauty,
The treacherous lips, the loving eyes –
And yet again you feel the fire

И как-то весело и больно
Тревожить язвы старых ран…
Тогда пишу. Диктует совесть,
Пером сердитый водит ум:
То соблазнительная повесть
Сокрытых дел и тайных дум;
Картины хладные разврата,
Преданья глупых юных дней,
Давно без пользы и возврата
Погибших в омуте страстей,
Средь битв незримых, но упорных,
Среди обманщиц и невежд,
Среди сомнений ложно-черных
И ложно-радужных надежд.
Судья безвестный и случайный,
Не дорожа чужою тайной,
Приличьем скрашенный порок
Я смело предаю позору;
Неумолим я и жесток…
Но, право, этих горьких строк
Неприготовленному взору
Я не решуся показать…
Скажите ж мне, о чем писать?..

К чему толпы неблагодарной
Мне злость и ненависть навлечь,
Чтоб бранью назвали коварной
Мою пророческую речь?
Чтоб тайный яд страницы знойной
Смутил ребенка сон покойный
И сердце слабое увлек
В свой необузданный поток?
О нет! преступною мечтою
Не ослепляя мысль мою,
Такой тяжелою ценою
Я вашей славы не куплю.

And know the strange and painful pleasure
Of probing wounds ill-healed by time…
At times like these I write, as conscience
And ancient anger guide my pen:
Sometimes it is the tempting romance
Of secret dealings, hidden plans;
Cold pictures of debauchery,
Stories of youthful days of madness
Now wasted irretrievably
And pointlessly in passion's maelstrom,
Amid the hidden headstrong battles,
The treacherous women and the dupes,
Amid the falsely doubting darkness
And the false rainbows of my hopes.
An unknown judge ordained by chance,
Not caring about people's secrets,
I boldly pillory the vices
That lurk beneath a seemly mask;
Implacable and fierce I am…
But still I cannot bring myself
To show this acrimonious verse
To the poor reader's childlike eyes…
So tell me then, what can I write?

Why should I pull down on my shoulders
The crowd's ignoble enmity
And let them call the prophet's voice
A crafty piece of calumny?
Why let the hell that haunts my lines
Scorch the calm slumber of a child
Or carry off my feeble readers
In the wild tumult of their waters?
No! no! I will not let my vision
Be blinded by this wicked dream,
With such a heavy price to reckon
I say no to your hall of fame.

translated by Peter France

[This poem echoes Pushkin's poem of 1824, 'Conversation of a Bookseller and a Poet', a disillusioned meditation on inspiration and commerce.]

Пленный рыцарь

Молча сижу под окошком темницы;
Синее небо отсюда мне видно:
В небе играют всё вольные птицы;
Глядя на них, мне и больно и стыдно.

Нет на устах моих грешной молитвы,
Нету ни песни во славу любезной:
Помню я только старинные битвы,
Меч мой тяжелый да панцирь железный.

В каменный панцирь я ныне закован,
Каменный шлем мою голову давит,
Щит мой от стрел и меча заколдован,
Конь мой бежит, и никто им не правит.

Быстрое время – мой конь неизменный,
Шлема забрало – решетка бойницы,
Каменный панцирь – высокие стены,
Щит мой – чугунные двери темницы.

Мчись же быстрее, летучее время!
Душно под новой бронею мне стало!
Смерть, как приедем, подержит мне стремя;
Слезу и сдерну с лица я забрало.

The Captive Knight

I sit at the prison window, silent;
I can see the azure sky,
Where all the free birds are playing;
I feel shame and misery.

No sinner's prayer on my lips,
No song to praise the beloved:
I recall only ancient wars,
I wear iron, my sword is heavy.

I am set in armour of stone,
Stone helmet crushing my head.
My shield bears a charm against arrows and swords,
No-one checks my galloping steed.

Racing time is my changeless steed,
The grille of my cell my visor,
My armour these high stone walls,
My shield the gates of my prison.

Flying time, race still faster!
I'll stifle in this coat of mail!
Death will hold my stirrup when we get there,
And I'll tear the helm from my face.

translated by Peter France

К портрету

Как мальчик кудрявый, резва,
Нарядна, как бабочка летом;
Значенья пустого слова
В устах ее полны приветом.

Ей нравиться долго нельзя:
Как цепь ей несносна привычка,
Она ускользнет, как змея,
Порхнет и умчится, как птичка.

Таит молодое чело
По воле – и радость и горе.
В глазах – как на небе светло,
В душе ее темно, как в море!

То истиной дышит в ней все,
То все в ней притворно и ложно!
Понять невозможно ее,
Зато не любить невозможно.

Portrait

She larks like a curly-haired boy,
Is elegant as a butterfly in summer;
And words that have no sense at all
On *her* lips are brimming with wonder.
Oh, no-one can please her for long:
She can't bear the binding of habit,
She glides away like a snake,
Or flitters and bobs like a linnet.
Her delicate brow conceals
Both sorrow and joy as she chooses.
Her eyes a blink of the sky overhead,
Her spirit dark tide as it races!
Now everything in her breathes truth,
And now it's all faking and feigning!
Impossible to grasp what she means,
Impossible not to be smitten.

translated by Alexander Hutchison

Завещание

Наедине с тобою, брат,
Хотел бы я побыть:
На свете мало, говорят,
Мне остается жить!
Поедешь скоро ты домой:
Смотри ж… Да что? моей судьбой,
Сказать по правде, очень
Никто не озабочен.

А если спросит кто-нибудь…
Ну, кто бы ни спросил,
Скажи им, что навылет в грудь
Я пулей ранен был,
Что умер честно за царя,
Что плохи наши лекаря
И что родному краю
Поклон я посылаю.

Отца и мать мою едва ль
Застанешь ты в живых…
Признаться, право, было б жаль
Мне опечалить их;
Но если кто из них и жив,
Скажи, что я писать ленив.
Что полк в поход послали
И чтоб меня не ждали.

Соседка есть у них одна…
Как вспомнишь, как давно
Расстались!.. Обо мне она
Не спросит… все равно,
Ты расскажи всю правду ей,
Пустого сердца не жалей;
Пускай она поплачет…
Ей ничего не значит!

Last Will

I want to be alone with you
Just for a minute, son;
If what they tell me here is true,
This is my lot, I'm done.
You'll soon be heading home again,
So look out... oh, why bother, when
No-one will worry greatly
What happened to me lately.

But if somebody wants to know,
Tell them – and all the rest –
That one day in a sortie I
Was shot right through the chest,
That here I'm dying for the tsar,
That medics aren't much good in war,
And that I send my greeting
To the country I grew up in.

You'll never find my father or
My mother still alive...
And I'd be sorry if my words
Made them feel sad, but if
By any chance one of them's left,
Tell them that I've no time to write,
The regiment's been posted –
Not to expect me home soon.

But there's a girl next door to them...
It seems ages ago
We parted... she won't ask for me...
But never mind, even so
Tell her the story from the start,
Don't try to spare her empty heart;
Let her cry all she pleases...
It's nothing to her really!

translated by Peter France

Родина

Люблю отчизну я, но странною любовью!
Не победит ее рассудок мой.
Ни слава, купленная кровью,
Ни полный гордого доверия покой,
Ни темной старины заветные преданья
Не шевелят во мне отрадного мечтанья.

Но я люблю – за что, не знаю сам –
Ее степей холодное молчанье,
Ее лесов безбрежных колыханье,
Разливы рек ее, подобные морям;
Проселочным путем люблю скакать в телеге
И, взором медленным пронзая ночи тень,
Встречать по сторонам, вздыхая о ночлеге,
Дрожащие огни печальных деревень;
Люблю дымок спаленной жнивы,
В степи ночующий обоз
И на холме средь желтой нивы
Чету белеющих берез.
С отрадой, многим незнакомой,
Я вижу полное гумно,
Избу, покрытую соломой,
С резными ставнями окно;
И в праздник, вечером росистым,
Смотреть до полночи готов
На пляску с топаньем и свистом
Под говор пьяных мужичков.

Ma Kintra

Ah lo'e ma kintra wi a fremmit luve,
That kythes nae rhyme or raison intil it,
Nae bluidy glorie bocht wi mailit gluive,
Nor peace that in prood confidence wis steepit,
Nor aa thae fand tradeetions o the past,
Can naethin steir ma hairt an haud it fast.

But yet ah lo'e, fir why ah canna say,
Her cranreuch plains hapt in an icy seelence,
The swey o boondless forests in her hielants,
Her rivers in a soom, lik seas, in spate.
Lowpie fir spang doun some cairt-road ah'll hie,
An glower slaely throu the mirk o nicht,
In howps tae spy some cot whaur ah micht stey,
Then glimpse some dowie clachan glentin bricht.
Ah lo'e the dwaiblie reek o burnin stibble,
A string o cairts stuid in the steppe at nicht,
Whiles stuid atop a cornfield in its middle,
A pair o bonnie birk trees gleamin bricht.
Wi pleasuir that is unbekent tae mony,
Ah see a weel-stockt granzie plenisht fairly,
A cot-hoose theakt wi strae that's trig an bonnie,
Wi shutters cairved o wuid hung oan its windaes.
Whiles at the kirn upon a dewy evenin,
Ah'll hunker doun tae watch the dance til twal,
Wi aa its splores its dancing an its whistlin,
Tae hear the drucken fowk enjoy theirsel.

translated by Rab Wilson

kintra country; *lo'e* love; *fremmit* strange; *kythes* reveals; *mailit* chain-mailed; *steepit* steeped; *fand* fond; *steir* stir; *cranreuch* frozen; *hapt* wrapped; *boondless* boundless; *soom* swim; *lowpie fir spang* in headlong dash; *slaely* slowly; *howps* hopes; *dowie* gloomy; *clachan* hamlet, village; *glentin* glinting; *dwaiblie* feeble, faint; *reek* smoke; *stibble* stubble; *unbekent* unknown; *granzie* granary; *theakt* thatched; *strae* straw; *trig* neat; *kirn* harvest festival; *hunker* squat; *twal* twelve; *splores* japes; *drucken* drunken

Последнее новоселье

Меж тем как Франция, среди рукоплесканий
И кликов радостных, встречает хладный прах
Погибшего давно среди немых страданий
   В изгнанье мрачном и цепях;
Меж тем как мир услужливой хвалою
Венчает позднего раскаянья порыв
И вздорная толпа, довольная собою,
   Гордится, прошлое забыв, –
Негодованию и чувству дав свободу,
Поняв тщеславие сих праздничных забот,
Мне хочется сказать великому народу:
   Ты жалкий и пустой народ!
Ты жалок потому, что вера, слава, гений,
Все, все великое, священное земли,
С насмешкой глупою ребяческих сомнений
   Тобой растоптано в пыли.
Из славы сделал ты игрушку лицемерья,
Из вольности – орудье палача,
И все заветные отцовские поверья
   Ты им рубил, рубил сплеча, –
Ты погибал… и он явился, с строгим взором,
Отмеченный божественным перстом,
И признан за вождя всеобщим приговором,
   И ваша жизнь слилася в нем, –
И вы окрепли вновь в тени его державы,
И мир трепещущий в безмолвии взирал
На ризу чудную могущества и славы,
   Которой вас он одевал.
Один, – он был везде, холодный, неизменный,
Отец седых дружин, любимый сын молвы,
В степях египетских, у стен покорной Вены,
   В снегах пылающей Москвы!

The Final Welcome Home

France sends out waves of happy applause,
To welcome these cold ashes, what's left
Of the man who in silence and sorrow, died
        Long ago, lonely, in exile, bereft.
The French mob's bloated, flattering praise
Comes to climax in this, all smug and inane,
In proud lamentations for what they don't know,
        Ignoring the past in their ghastly refrain.
I want to rage and roar upon them,
To cry that this national joy is all vain,
All festivities foolish, the mob merely selfish,
        Crass and banal. My contempt gives me pain.
I pity you. All that earth makes noble and dear –
Faith, genius, the sacred, the great and the just –
With a sickening, puerile, ignorant sneer,
        You've stamped your grimy feet upon, and trampled
                        in the dust.

Freedom, honour, everything beloved of
Your mothers, fathers, kin, for generations back,
You have made into nothing but frivolous toys
        For your hypocritical hands to crack.
You were nearly dead when he first appeared,
Looking grim, determined, destined to act.
You praised him and raised him to lead you,
        Coming together, supporting him, in a grand, united
                        pact.

Beneath his command you grew strong, once again.
The world was silent and scared, thinking
Of the presence of power and the grandeur of men
        He gave you. He stared on unblinking,
Always alone, wherever he was, and cool,
Father beloved of battalions, dear son of all glory to come –
In Egypt's deserts, by Vienna's broken wall,
        In burning Moscow's ruins and the endless snowfall.

А вы что делали, скажите, в это время,
Когда в полях чужих он гордо погибал?
Вы потрясали власть избранную, как бремя,
 Точили в темноте кинжал!
Среди последних битв, отчаянных усилий,
В испуге не поняв позора своего,
Как женщина, ему вы изменили
 И, как рабы, вы предали его!
Лишенный прав и места гражданина,
Разбитый свой венец он снял и бросил сам,
И вам оставил он в залог родного сына –
 Вы сына выдали врагам!
Тогда, отяготив позорными цепями,
Героя увезли от плачущих дружин,
И на чужой скале, за синими морями,
 Забытый, он угас один –
Один, – замучен мщением бесплодным,
Безмолвною и гордою тоской –
И как простой солдат в плаще своем походном
 Зарыт наемною рукой.

*

Но годы протекли, и ветреное племя
Кричит: «Подайте нам священный этот прах!
Он наш; его теперь, великой жатвы семя,
 Зароем мы в спасенных им стенах!»
И возвратился он на родину; безумно,
Как прежде, вкруг него теснятся и бегут
И в пышный гроб, среди столицы шумной,
 Остатки тленные кладут.
Желанье позднее увенчано успехом!
И краткий свой восторг сменив уже другим,
Гуляя, топчет их с самодовольным смехом
 Толпа, дрожавшая пред ним.

*

So tell me, what did you do with your lives,
When he faced down death in such foreigners' lands?
You drained every drop of his power away
      And secretly sharpened your knives.
In his final battle and desperate trial
You were scared of your own betrayal,
Like a woman who lies though her husband is loyal,
      Like slaves in their own denial.
Citizen no longer, no status remaining,
His crown was cracked, so he tossed it, disdaining,
But left you his son, a pledge of faith, so —
      And you handed him over to the old mortal foe.
Then under the weight of chains of shame,
From the mournful troops the hero was taken
To an alien rock in a far blue sea, where
      He entered oblivion, dying forsaken.
Alone, in his torture, he starved for revenge,
In his anguish, intense, silent and proud.
He was buried then, like a soldier, simply,
      By a hired man, in a military shroud.

★

Years passed. The fickle nation screamed:
'Return to us his ashes, here where he belongs!
We should bury him among us, for his seed has given
      Harvest. He should rest in the place he redeemed.'
Returned to his homeland, the mob crowded round
His earthly remains, placed, in a glorious tomb,
The silent heart of the nation's clamorous sound,
      In the capital's centre, a quiet room.
The wish that came too late is granted.
The crowd, capriciously, moves elsewhere,
Getting keen on something else,
      Who trembled when he was there.

★

И грустно мне, когда подумаю, что ныне
Нарушена святая тишина
Вокруг того, кто ждал в своей пустыне
Так жадно, столько лет спокойствия и сна!
И если дух вождя примчится на свиданье
С гробницей новою, где прах его лежит,
  Какое в нем негодованье
  При этом виде закипит!
Как будет он жалеть, печалию томимый,
О знойном острове, под небом дальних стран,
Где сторожил его, как он непобедимый,
  Как он великий, океан!

And I am saddened by this thought:
You break the sacred silence I would keep
Around him who, for years, had waited for
      An end to his torment, in peace, rest and sleep.
Imagine, though: his hero's spirit flies
To this sepulchral shrine
Where his ashes still remain –
      What anger fires him up again!
But then old grief would strike, he'd recall
The sweaty, sweltering island, under its distant sky
And the vast, invincible ocean surrounding
      Him, proved his equal, eternally confounding!

translated by Alan Riach

[In 1840, during the reign of Louis-Philippe, the remains of Napoleon, who
had died on St Helena in 1821, were brought back to France for a state funeral.]

* * *

Прощай, немытая Россия,
Страна рабов, страна господ,
И вы, мундиры голубые,
И ты, им преданный народ.

Быть может, за стеной Кавказа
Сокроюсь от твоих пашей,
От их всевидящего глаза,
От их всеслышащих ушей.

'Unwasht Russia, fare ye weel'

Unwasht Russia, fare ye weel,
Kintra o slaves an sovereigns,
O licht blue polis uniforms,
An ye, the fowk that's tae thaim leal.

Aiblins ayont the Caucasus wa,
Ah'll frae yer Pashas derne awa,
Frae thae gleg een that aye see aa,
Thae lugs that miss naethin ava.

translated by Rab Wilson

'Farewell, soap-dodging Russia'

Farewell, soap-dodging Russia,
Slaveland of tsarinas and tsars;
Farewell, Bad Cop, blue as Prussia,
And yon mobs of slobs licking your arse.

Maybe way beyond the Caucasus
And your Vlad lads, free as a bird,
I'll give the slip to those all-seeing eyes,
Those jug-ears that don't miss a word.

translated by Robert Crawford

Сон

В полдневный жар в долине Дагестана
С свинцом в груди лежал недвижим я;
Глубокая еще дымилась рана,
По капле кровь точилася моя.

Лежал один я на песке долины;
Уступы скал теснилися кругом,
И солнце жгло их желтые вершины
И жгло меня – но спал я мертвым сном.

И снился мне сияющий огнями
Вечерний пир в родимой стороне.
Меж юных жен, увенчанных цветами,
Шел разговор веселый обо мне.

Но, в разговор веселый не вступая,
Сидела там задумчиво одна,
И в грустный сон душа ее младая
Бог знает чем была погружена;

И снилась ей долина Дагестана;
Знакомый труп лежал в долине той;
В его груди, дымясь, чернела рана,
И кровь лилась хладеющей струей.

A Dream

In the noon heat in a valley in Daghestan
I lay unmoving, a bullet in my chest;
Steam was still rising from the deep wound,
And drop by drop the blood was seeping out.

I lay alone on the valley's sandy floor,
Walled in by jutting cliffs on every side;
The sun was scorching their yellow pinnacles
And scorching me, but I slept like the dead.

And in a dream I saw the brilliant glow
Of a gala evening in my native land.
Young women with festive garlands in their hair
Were talking about me in a merry band.

But there was one who sat alone and thought
And took no part in all the merry chat,
And her young soul was plunged in a sad dream,
Distracted from the ball by God knows what;

And in a dream in a valley in Daghestan
She saw a familiar corpse stretched on the ground;
A steaming wound lay darkly on his chest,
And the blood that seeped from it was growing cold.

translated by Peter France

* * *

Выхожу один я на дорогу;
Сквозь туман кремнистый путь блестит;
Ночь тиха. Пустыня внемлет богу,
И звезда с звездою говорит.

В небесах торжественно и чудно!
Спит земля в сиянье голубом…
Что же мне так больно и так трудно?
Жду ль чего? Жалею ли о чем?

Уж не жду от жизни ничего я,
И не жаль мне прошлого ничуть;
Я ищу свободы и покоя!
Я б хотел забыться и заснуть!

Но не тем холодным сном могилы…
Я б желал навеки так заснуть,
Чтоб в груди дремали жизни силы,
Чтоб, дыша, вздымалась тихо грудь;

Чтоб всю ночь, весь день мой слух лелея,
Про любовь мне сладкий голос пел,
Надо мной чтоб, вечно зеленея,
Темный дуб склонялся и шумел.

Night-Walk

I come out alone onto the boreen,
A flinty path glimmering through mist,
Stilly night, wilderness listening to God,
The constellations in conversation,

Astonishing things up there in the sky,
The earth dozing in pale-blue radiance.
Why, then, am I so downhearted? What
Am I waiting for? What do I regret?

I've stopped expecting anything from life,
I don't feel nostalgic about the past,
I long for freedom and tranquillity,
I long for forgetfulness and sleep,

But not the grave's spine-chilling coma.
I would prefer to fall asleep for ever
With the life force snoozing in my breast
As it rises and falls imperceptibly,

Night and day a kind voice soothing my ears
With affectionate lullabies about love
And over me, green for eternity,
A shadowy oak leaning and rustling.

translated by Michael Longley

Морская царевна

В море царевич купает коня;
Слышит: «Царевич! взгляни на меня!»

Фыркает конь и ушами прядет,
Брызжет и плещет и дале плывет.

Слышит царевич: «Я царская дочь!
Хочешь провесть ты с царевною ночь?»

Вот показалась рука из воды,
Ловит за кисти шелковой узды.

Вышла младая потом голова,
В косу вплелася морская трава.

Синие очи любовью горят;
Брызги на шее, как жемчуг, дрожат.

Мыслит царевич: «Добро же! постой!»
За косу ловко схватил он рукой.

Держит, рука боевая сильна:
Плачет и молит и бьется она.

К берегу витязь отважно плывет;
Выплыл; товарищей громко зовет:

«Эй, вы! сходитесь, лихие друзья!
Гляньте, как бьется добыча моя…

Что ж вы стоите смущенной толпой?
Али красы не видали такой?»

Вот оглянулся царевич назад:
Ахнул! померк торжествующий взгляд.

Tsarévna of the Sea

Inti the swaws the prince maun ride;
He hears a voice within the tide.

Snirtin, its lang lugs fidgin fain,
His cuddy splatters through the faem.

Thon voice: 'I am a sea-king's quine:
Come, prince, this nicht you sall be mine.'

A slim haun raxed oot o the sea:
Caucht the silk-bridle b' its toorie;

A young heid rose oot o the wet,
The sea-ware fankled in its plet.

Love burns in her daurk-blue een,
Her neck dreeps wi a pearly sheen.

Tsarévich ponders: 'Here! Haud on!'
Nabs her hair wi juist ae haun,

He grups her wi his sodger's micht:
She greets, begs, chauves against her plicht.

Oor big lawd swims back ti the strand,
Climbs oot, cries ti his warrior band,

'Hey, fellaes! Gaither roun, and quick!
My mermaid here, she's got some kick!

'Why d'ye staund bumbazed, and stare?
She's a wee stotter, that's fir shair!'

Juist then, Tsarévich looked ahint,
Swore: fir his victory wis tint.

Видит, лежит на песке золотом
Чудо морское с зеленым хвостом;

Хвост чешуею змеиной покрыт,
Весь замирая, свиваясь, дрожит;

Пена струями сбегает с чела,
Очи одела смертельная мгла.

Бледные руки хватают песок;
Шепчут уста непонятный упрек…

Едет царевич задумчиво прочь,
Будет он помнить про царскую дочь!

Upon thon gowden strand, he's seen
A ferlie wi a tail o green,

Happit wi serpens' scales, there leein,
Tremmlin, writhin, near ti deein,

Faem streams frae her bonny brou,
Mirk are her een wi the cauld grue.

Pale fingers gruppin saund, hou faint
Upon her lips, her whuspered plaint…

The prince rides, thinks ti whit he'd brocht her.
He'll no forget the sea-king's dochter!

translated by Tom Hubbard

swaws waves; *maun* must; *snirtin* snorting; *fidgin fain* restlessly eager;
cuddy horse; *thon* that; *quine* girl; *haun* hand; *raxed* reached; *toorie* tassel;
sea-ware seaweed; *fankled* tangled; *plet* braid; *dreeps* drips; *sodger's*
soldier's; *greets* weeps; *chauves* chafes; *bumbazed* confused; *stotter* a
stunner (said of a woman); *shair* sure; *ahint* behind; *tint* lost; *ferlie* marvel;
happit covered; *deein* dying; *grue* horror

Листок

Дубовый листок оторвался от ветки родимой
И в степь укатился, жестокою бурей гонимый;
Засох и увял он от холода, зноя и горя
И вот, наконец, докатился до Черного моря.

У Черного моря чинара стоит молодая;
С ней шепчется ветер, зеленые ветви лаская;
На ветвях зеленых качаются райские птицы;
Поют они песни про славу морской царь-девицы.

И странник прижался у корня чинары высокой;
Приюта на время он молит с тоскою глубокой,
И так говорит он: «Я бедный листочек дубовый,
До срока созрел я и вырос в отчизне суровой.

Один и без цели по свету ношуся давно я,
Засох я без тени, увял я без сна и покоя.
Прими же пришельца меж листьев своих изумрудных,
Немало я знаю рассказов мудреных и чудных.»

«На что мне тебя? – отвечает младая чинара, –
Ты пылен и желт, – и сынам моим свежим не пара.
Ты много видал – да к чему мне твои небылицы?
Мой слух утомили давно уж и райские птицы.

Иди себе дальше; о странник! тебя я не знаю!
Я солнцем любима, цвету для него и блистаю;
По небу я ветви раскинула здесь на просторе,
И корни мои умывает холодное море.»

The Leaf

An oak leaf ripped itself free of its native branch.
Buffeted by raging storms, it took its chances.
But the steppe withered it with cold, heat and sorrow.
Even so, its faded form hollowed a furrow

As far as the Black Sea, where a sycamore stands –
A young sycamore caressed by the warm hands
Of the whispering wind. Sleek, celestial birds
Sway to the rhythm of its green branches. The words

Of their songs tell of a beautiful princess
Who lives below the sea. The wanderer presses
Himself against the root of the tall sycamore:
He prays for a moment's shelter. Heart-sore,

This is what he says: 'I'm a poor little oak leaf,
One who matured early and whose singular grief
Was to grow up in a harsh land and then – but why? –
To wander this world alone. Without shade, I dried.

Without sleep and peace, I faded. But I know
Many strange and wonderful tales, if only you
Would take this stranger among your emerald leaves.'
'What need have I of you?' the young sycamore breathes.

'Dusty and yellowed – no match for my fresh offspring.
You've seen much, I'll grant, but of what you might sing,
I've little need. Long ago, I even tired
Of the singing of these otherworldly birds.

Go on your way, traveller, you're no friend of mine.
I am loved by the sun. For him, I bloom and shine.
I have spread my branches across the open sky
And my roots are washed by the indifferent sea.'

translated by Tom Pow

Пророк

С тех пор как вечный судия
Мне дал всеведенье пророка,
В очах людей читаю я
Страницы злобы и порока.

Провозглашать я стал любви
И правды чистые ученья:
В меня все ближние мои
Бросали бешено каменья.

Посыпал пеплом я главу,
Из городов бежал я нищий,
И вот в пустыне я живу,
Как птицы, даром божьей пищи;

Завет предвечного храня,
Мне тварь покорна там земная;
И звезды слушают меня,
Лучами радостно играя.

Когда же через шумный град
Я пробираюсь торопливо,
То старцы детям говорят
С улыбкою самолюбивой:

«Смотрите: вот пример для вас!
Он горд был, не ужился с нами:
Глупец, хотел уверить нас,
Что бог гласит его устами!

Смотрите ж, дети, на него:
Как он угрюм, и худ, и бледен!
Смотрите, как он наг и беден,
Как презирают все его!»

The Prophet

Since God forever dropped on me
The vision of future evidence,
The eyes of everyone I see
Are fixed stares of malevolence.

I set out to speak of what was love,
Truth, the essence, of learning and help
But everyone suddenly started to shove,
Stone and skelp

Me. I ran. I left the cities all
Behind me, with nothing, set out, lonely, driven,
For the deserts, and there in the desolate hall
Of God, I live now, on whatever is given.

I keep the pact – the world is good –
The animals still, to me, attentive –
The starlight sings in solitude
Glimmers and shines, playful, reflective.

But when I go back to the roaring town,
I hurry through, I don't loaf or linger,
For old folk at their children frown
And say with lifted pointing finger:

'Mark that man! He's one to watch!
He wouldn't conform, an awkward sod –
He tried to tell us, make us catch
His meaning, as if it was ordained by God!

'Look at him, children, look at him now –
Ragged, lean – he is restless and fated,
Never at ease, his furrowed brow –
Scorn him, despise him, let him be hated!'

translated by Alan Riach

* * *

Никто моим словам не внемлет… я один.
День гаснет… красными рисуясь полосами,
На запад уклонились тучи, и камин
Трещит передо мной. Я полон весь мечтами
О будущем… и дни мои толпой
Однообразною проходят предо мной,
И тщетно я ищу смущенными очами
Меж них хоть день один, отмеченный судьбой!

'Nobody will hear these words'

Nobody will hear these words. I stand alone, the isolated man.
And the long day's snuffing out at last, the sky's red flames are
                              streaked across the dark.
The evening's clouds go into the west and the embers of the day
Are crackles and sparks in the dying hearth before me.
I'm dreaming of what is to come. My days in a dreary crowd
                              fall
Into line, parade themselves before me to infinity.
My dim, bewildered eyes are hopeless, eager, searching
                              through them all,
For one – just one – made significant by fate!

translated by Alan Riach

Валерик

Я к вам пишу случайно; право,
Не знаю как и для чего.
Я потерял уж это право.
И что скажу вам? – ничего!
Что помню вас? – но, боже правый,
Вы это знаете давно;
И вам, конечно, все равно.

И знать вам также нету нужды,
Где я? что я? в какой глуши?
Душою мы друг другу чужды,
Да вряд ли есть родство души.
Страницы прошлого читая,
Их по порядку разбирая
Теперь остынувшим умом,
Разуверяюсь я во всем.
Смешно же сердцем лицемерить
Перед собою столько лет;
Добро б еще морочить свет!
Да и притом, что пользы верить
Тому, чего уж больше нет?..
Безумно ждать любви заочной?
В наш век все чувства лишь на срок;
Но я вас помню – да и точно,
Я вас никак забыть не мог!

Во-первых, потому, что много
И долго, долго вас любил,
Потом страданьем и тревогой
За дни блаженства заплатил;
Потом в раскаянье бесплодном
Влачил я цепь тяжелых лет
И размышлением холодным
Убил последний жизни цвет.
С людьми сближаясь осторожно,
Забыл я шум младых проказ,
Любовь, поэзию, – но вас
Забыть мне было невозможно.

Valerik

I don't know really how it happens
Or why, that I am writing now.
I've lost the right to send you letters –
And what have I got to say to you?
That I remember...? God almighty!
You've known that now for many years,
And naturally, you don't care.

Nor do you need to know in detail
How I am living, where I've gone.
Our souls are strangers to each other –
But are there any kindred souls?
As I look over bygone days
And with a mind that's lost its fervour
Run through them one after another,
I feel belief slipping away.
Ridiculous, all that play-acting
Just for yourself, year after year!
All right if you can fool the public,
But even then, what use believing
In things that now have disappeared?...
It's mad to seek love at a distance.
Today's emotions soon decline;
But I remember you – and truly
I couldn't drive you from my mind!

Firstly because I loved you deeply
For many, many years, and then
Because I later paid in worry
And suffering for that happiness;
After that in vain repentance
I dragged the heavy chain of time
And with an artificial coldness
Killed off the last spark of life.
I moved with caution among people,
Forgot my noisy headstrong youth
And love and poetry, but never
Let go the memory of you.

И к мысли этой я привык,
Мой крест несу я без роптанья:
То иль другое наказанье?
Не все ль одно. Я жизнь постиг;
Судьбе, как турок иль татарин,
За все я ровно благодарен;
У бога счастья не прошу
И молча зло переношу.
Быть может, небеса Востока
Меня с ученьем их пророка
Невольно сблизили. Притом
И жизнь всечасно кочевая,
Труды, заботы ночь и днем,
Все, размышлению мешая,
Приводит в первобытный вид
Больную душу: сердце спит,
Простора нет воображенью…
И нет работы голове…
Зато лежишь в густой траве
И дремлешь под широкой тенью
Чинар иль виноградных лоз,
Кругом белеются палатки;
Казачьи тощие лошадки
Стоят рядком, повеся нос;
У медных пушек спит прислуга.
Едва дымятся фитили;
Попарно цепь стоит вдали;
Штыки горят под солнцем юга.
Вот разговор о старине
В палатке ближней слышен мне;
Как при Ермолове ходили
В Чечню, в Аварию, к горам;
Как там дрались, как мы их били,
Как доставалося и нам;
И вижу я неподалеку
У речки, следуя пророку,
Мирной татарин свой намаз
Творит, не подымая глаз;
А вот кружком сидят другие.

I've grown accustomed to this thought,
I bear my cross without complaining:
Which punishment awaits me now?
What difference does it make? I know
What life is, like a Turk I'm thankful
For everything fate heaps upon me;
In silence I endure misfortune
And don't ask God for happiness.
Perhaps life under eastern skies
Unknowingly made me more ready
To hear the prophet's word. And then
The wandering life that I've been leading,
Labours and cares both night and day
And everything that stops you thinking –
All bring the free soul to the state
Of nature, and the heart feels nothing,
Imagination is confined…
There's nothing to exert your mind,
But you can lie in the long grass
Or slumber in the spreading shadow
With rows of white tents all around you;
Close by, the skinny Cossack horses
Stand with a melancholy air,
The gunners doze by the bronze cannons.
The fuses are still smoking; there,
Far off, you see two lines of soldiers
With bayonets flaming in the sun.
And in the nearby tents they're telling
Stories of the old days, how once
With Yermolov in charge we marched
Through mountains, Chechnya and Avaria,
And fought there, how we beat their armies
And took a beating too. I see
Not far away, down by the river,
A peaceful Tartar at his prayers,
Following the prophet's rules, not raising
His eyes to look around, and here
Are others sitting in a circle.

Люблю я цвет их желтых лиц,
Подобный цвету ноговиц,
Их шапки, рукава худые,
Их темный и лукавый взор
И их гортанный разговор.
Чу - дальний выстрел! Прожужжала
Шальная пуля… славный звук…
Вот крик – и снова все вокруг
Затихло… Но жара уж спала,
Ведут коней на водопой,
Зашевелилася пехота;
Вот проскакал один, другой!
Шум, говор. Где вторая рота?
Что, вьючить? – что же капитан?
Повозки выдвигайте живо!
«Савельич!» – «Ой ли!» – «Дай огниво!»
Подъем ударил барабан –
Гудит музыка полковая;
Между колоннами въезжая,
Звенят орудья. Генерал
Вперед со свитой поскакал…
Рассыпались в широком поле,
Как пчелы, с гиком казаки;
Уж показалися значки
Там на опушке – два, и боле.
А вот в чалме один мюрид
В черкеске красной ездит важно,
Конь светло-серый весь кипит,
Он машет, кличет – где отважный?
Кто выдет с ним на смертный бой!..
Сейчас, смотрите: в шапке черной
Казак пустился гребенской;
Винтовку выхватил проворно,
Уж близко… выстрел… легкий дым…
Эй вы, станичники, за ним…
Что? ранен!.. – Ничего, безделка… –
И завязалась перестрелка…

Но в этих сшибках удалых

I love the colour of their skin
Yellow as the ribbons on their coats,
Their caps, their narrow sleeves, their sombre
And crafty-looking eyes, the rough
Sounds of their guttural conversations.
Listen! a distant shot... The bullet
Whistles close by... a splendid sound...
And then a shout – then all goes quiet
Again... the midday heat abates,
They lead the horses to the water.
The infantry begins to move;
One man comes galloping... another!
Noise, voices... where's B Company?
Should we be saddling? Where's the captain?
Bring out the wagons at the double!
'Savelich!' 'What?' 'Quick, bring a flint!'
The drum beats for the troops to march –
The regimental band is playing;
The cannons clatter as they pass
Between the lines of men. The general
Has galloped forward with his staff...
With their wild war-whoops now the Cossacks
Spread out over the field like bees;
There, at the forest edge, the ensigns
Are visible – two, three or more...
Then in a red Circassian tunic
A turbaned Muslim gallops up
Sitting a fiery light-grey steed,
Waving and shouting: where's the champion
Who dares meet him in single combat!...
And straight away, a Greben Cossack
In a black cap comes darting out
With rifle at the ready... now
He's up with him... a bang... smoke drifting...
Hey you, his comrades, get in there...
What's that? He's wounded? – Just a scratch... –
And then the shooting starts in earnest...

But in these warlike skirmishes

Забавы много, толку мало;
Прохладным вечером, бывало
Мы любовалися на них,
Без кровожадного волненья,
Как на трагический балет;
Зато видал я представленья,
Каких у вас на сцене нет…

Раз – это было под Гихами –
Мы проходили темный лес;
Огнем дыша, пылал над нами
Лазурно-яркий свод небес.
Нам был обещан бой жестокий.
Из гор Ичкерии далекой
Уже в Чечню на братний зов
Толпы стекались удальцов.
Над допотопными лесами
Мелькали маяки кругом;
И дым их то вился столпом,
То расстилался облаками;
И оживилися леса;
Скликались дико голоса
Под их зелеными шатрами.
Едва лишь выбрался обоз
В поляну, дело началось;
Чу! в арьергард орудья просят;
Вот ружья из кустов выносят,
Вот тащат за ноги людей
И кличут громко лекарей;
А вот и слева, из опушки,
Вдруг с гиком кинулись па пушки;
И градом пуль с вершин дерев
Отряд осыпан. Впереди же
Все тихо – там между кустов
Бежал поток. Подходим ближе.
Пустили несколько гранат;
Еще подвинулись; молчат;
Но вот над бревнами завала
Ружье как будто заблистало;

There's fun, but not a lot of purpose;
Sometimes on a cool evening we
Would watch them with appreciation
Rather than blood-thirsty emotion,
As if they were some tragic dance.
But sometimes I saw a performance
Such as you'd never see at home…

One day – it wasn't far from Gikh –
Our troop was riding through the forest.
The hot breath of the clear blue sky
Was roasting us. We had been promised
A murderous fight. Into Chechnya
Out of Ishkeria's distant mountains
The warrior hordes of Muslim tribesmen
Were flooding to their brothers' aid.
High over the primeval forests
Beacons were flaming in the blue,
Their smoke now rising in a column,
Now spreading sideways in a cloud.
The forests had come to life; beneath
Their wide green canopies you heard
A wild cacophony of voices.
The wagon trains have barely reached
The clearing when the business starts;
Cannons are needed in the rear;
Out of the bushes muskets appear;
They're dragging off the wounded soldiers
And bellowing to send the doctors.
Then suddenly, out of the woods,
Some men come whooping at the guns;
From the treetops a hail of bullets
Lashes our squadron. But up front
All's quiet. There among the bushes
A stream is flowing. We ride up.
We let them have a few grenades,
Then we move on a bit…Dead silence.
But then over the barricade
We glimpse what seems to be a rifle;

Потом мелькнуло шапки две;
И вновь все спряталось в траве.
То было грозное молчанье,
Недолго длилося оно,
Но в этом странном ожиданье
Забилось сердце не одно.
Вдруг залп… глядим: лежат рядами,
Что нужды? здешние полки
Народ испытанный… «В штыки,
Дружнее!» – раздалось за нами.
Кровь загорелася в груди!
Все офицеры впереди…
Верхом помчался на завалы
Кто не успел спрыгнуть с коня…
«Ура!» – и смолкло. «Вон кинжалы,
В приклады!» – и пошла резня.
И два часа в струях потока
Бой длился. Резались жестоко,
Как звери, молча, с грудью грудь,
Ручей телами запрудили.
Хотел воды я зачерпнуть…
(И зной и битва утомили
Меня), но мутная волна
Была тепла, была красна.

На берегу, под тенью дуба,
Пройдя завалов первый ряд,
Стоял кружок. Один солдат
Был на коленах; мрачно, грубо
Казалось выраженье лиц,
Но слезы капали с ресниц,
Покрытых пылью… на шинели,
Спиною к дереву, лежал
Их капитан. Он умирал;
В груди его едва чернели
Две ранки; кровь его чуть-чуть
Сочилась. Но высоко грудь
И трудно подымалась, взоры
Бродили страшно, он шептал…

A couple of caps can just be seen,
Then vanish in the grass again.
The scene was ominously quiet,
But not for long, and as we lay
In sinister anticipation
Our hearts were thumping furiously.
A cannon shot... we look, take cover,
But what's the need? Our regiments
Are seasoned men... We hear the order:
'Together, lads! Fix bayonets!'
In every breast the blood is boiling!
The officers are all up ahead,
Some of them go riding at the barrier
While others manage to dismount...
'Hurrah!'... then silence. 'Watch their daggers,
Use butts!' A hand-to-hand broke out,
And for two hours the fight went on
Down in the river. Never speaking,
They fought like lions, face to face,
And bodies dammed the river's course.
Exhausted with the heat and fighting,
I wanted to collect some water,
But in the muddy river bed
The water was all warm and red.

Up on the bank beneath an oak-tree,
Beyond the nearest barricade
There was a group of men; a soldier
Was kneeling down, and every face
Was grim and coarse, but the warm tears
Were running from their dust-filled eyes.
Leaning against a tree, their captain
Was lying on an army greatcoat
And dying; on his chest two wounds
Showed black, and from them trickled blood.
His chest was rising high, then sinking
As with an effort he drew breath;
His eyes rolled fearfully around, he whispered:

«Спасите, братцы. Тащат в горы.
Постойте – ранен генерал…
Не слышат…» Долго он стонал,
Но все слабей, и понемногу
Затих и душу отдал богу;
На ружья опершись, кругом
Стояли усачи седые…
И тихо плакали… потом
Его остатки боевые
Накрыли бережно плащом
И понесли. Тоской томимый,
Им вслед смотрел я недвижимый.
Меж тем товарищей, друзей
Со вздохом возле называли;
Но не нашел в душе моей
Я сожаленья, ни печали.
Уже затихло все; тела
Стащили в кучу; кровь текла
Струею дымной по каменьям,
Ее тяжелым испареньем
Был полон воздух. Генерал
Сидел в тени на барабане
И донесенья принимал.
Окрестный лес, как бы в тумане,
Синел в дыму пороховом.
А там, вдали, грядой нестройной,
Но вечно гордой и спокойной,
Тянулись горы – и Казбек
Сверкал главой остроконечной.
И с грустью тайной и сердечной
Я думал: «Жалкий человек.
Чего он хочет!.. небо ясно,
Под небом места много всем,
Но беспрестанно и напрасно
Один враждует он-зачем?»
Галуб прервал мое мечтанье,
Ударив по плечу; он был
Кунак мой; я его спросил,
Как месту этому названье?

'Help me, my friends. They're going up.
Hold on a bit – the general's wounded...
Can't hear...' For ages he kept groaning,
But his voice weakened, slowed, then stopped,
And he gave up his soul to God.
All round him, leaning on their rifles,
The grey moustachioed soldiers wept
And didn't say a word; they covered
His body carefully with a cape.
I watched unmoving as they left
And felt my heart was gripped by sorrow.
Meanwhile the names of comrades, friends,
Were spoken with a sigh all round me,
But in my spirit I could feel
No sympathy for them, no grief.
Now all was quiet, and the bodies
Were piled into a heap, blood flowed
Over the stones, its smoky vapour
Weighed on the air. Beneath the shade
The general, sitting on a drum,
Was listening to reports. The forest
All round our camp seemed bathed in mist,
Drowning in a blue haze of powder.
But there, far off, the mountains towered,
Not shapely, but since days long dead
Tranquil and proud – Kazbek in power
Reared up his sparkling jagged head.
And with a secret, heart-felt pain
I wondered: 'Miserable men,
What do they want? The sky is cloudless,
There's room for all beneath the sky,
Yet ceaselessly and to no purpose
They war with one another – why?'
My musings were disturbed by Galub,
My Tartar friend–in–arms, who came
And clapped me on the back. I asked him:
'What do they call this place?' 'Its name,'

Он отвечал мне: «Валерик,
А перевесть на ваш язык,
Так будет речка смерти: верно,
Дано старинными людьми.»
«А сколько их дралось примерно
Сегодня?» – «Тысяч до семи.»
«А много горцы потеряли?»
«Как знать? – зачем вы не считали!»
«Да! будет, – кто-то тут сказал, –
Им в память эгот день кровавый!»
Чеченец посмотрел лукаво
И головою покачал.

Но я боюся вам наскучить,
В забавах света вам смешны
Тревоги дикие войны;
Свой ум вы не привыкли мучить
Тяжелой думой о конце;
На вашем молодом лице
Следов заботы и печали
Не отыскать, и вы едва ли
Вблизи когда-нибудь видали,
Как умирают. Дай вам бог
И не видать: иных тревог
Довольно есть. В самозабвенье
Не лучше ль кончить жизни путь?
И беспробудным сном заснуть
С мечтой о близком пробужденье?

Теперь прощайте: если вас
Мой безыскусственный рассказ
Развеселит, займет хоть малость,
Я буду счастлив. А не так?
Простите мне его как шалость
И тихо молвите: чудак!..

He said, 'is Valerik; translated
Into your language, that would mean
"River of death"; no doubt our fathers
In times gone by gave it this name.'
'How many men today d'you think
Were fighting here?' 'Maybe seven thousand.'
'And did they lose a lot, the tribesmen?'
'God knows! You should have counted them!'
And someone nearby said: 'This bloody
Day will be one they won't forget!'
The Chechen glanced at me obliquely
And with a sly look shook his head.

But I'm afraid of boring you
And that the savage sounds of war
Will seem odd in your social flurry.
You're not accustomed to the worry
Of gloomy thoughts of our last end.
On your young face it's hard to find
Traces of care or melancholy,
And I suppose that you will hardly
Be used to seeing people dying.
God grant you never have to see
Such things: without them there will be
Troubles enough. Is it not better
Unknowingly to tread the road
And then to fall asleep for good
With dreams of speedy resurrection?

Farewell now: if my artless tale
Has given you some entertainment
And filled your leisure for a while,
I shall be glad; if I'm mistaken,
Forgive this nonsense if you can
And gently murmur: what a man!...

translated by Peter France

[The battle on the River Valerik was one of the bloodiest of the 1840 campaign against the Chechens; Lermontov distinguished himself by his bravery in it.]

Notes on the Translators

Robert Crawford has published seven collections of poetry, including *A Scottish Assembly* (1990) and *Full Volume* (2008). With Mick Imlah he edited *The Penguin Book of Scottish Verse* (2000). His prose books include a biography of Robert Burns, *The Bard* (2009), and *Bannockburns: Scottish Independence and Literary Imagination* (2014). He is a professor in the School of English at the University of St Andrews.

Anna Crowe lives in St Andrews and is the co-founder and former Artistic Director of StAnza, Scotland's International Poetry Festival. Poet, creative writing tutor, and translator, mostly of Catalan and Mexican poetry, her poetry and translations have been Poetry Book Society Choices. Recent collections include *Figures in a Landscape* (2010) and a translation of Joan Margarit's poems, *Strangely Happy* (2011).

Colin Donati is a Scottish poet, musician and artist of third-generation Italian descent. He has edited the collected plays of Robert McLellan (1907–85), *Robert McLellan: Playing Scotland's Story* (Luath, 2013), and is completing a Scots translation, from the Russian, of Dostoevsky's *Crime and Punishment*. He lives in Edinburgh.

Sasha Dugdale is a poet and translator. Her translations of Russian contemporary drama have been staged by the Royal Court Theatre, the Royal Shakespeare Company and other theatres in the UK, the USA and Australia. Her collection of translations of Elena Shvarts was a Poetry Book Society Recommended Translation. She is editor of *Modern Poetry in Translation*.

Rose France teaches Russian literature and language at Edinburgh University and works as a freelance Russian translator and interpreter. She has been writing poetry and short stories for several years. In 2008 she won third prize in the English Association Fellows' Poetry Prize and she was shortlisted for the Bridport Prize (short story category) in 2010.

Tom Hubbard has been a Visiting Professor at the Universities of Budapest, Connecticut and Grenoble. His novel *Marie B.* (2008) is based on the life of the Ukrainian-born painter Marie Bashkirtseff, and a second novel, *The Lucky Charm of Major Bessop*, is due to appear in 2014. His recent poetry collections are *The Chagall Winnocks* (2011) and *Parapets and Labyrinths* (2013), both Grace Note Publications.

Alexander Hutchison lives in Glasgow, and writes in Scots and English. Recent collections are *Scales Dog: Poems New and Selected* (Salt, 2007) and *Bones & Breath* (Salt, 2013). His first book *Deep-Tap Tree* (University of Massachusetts Press, 1978) is still in print. www.alexanderhutchison.com

Michael Longley was born in Belfast, where he still lives, and studied classics at Trinity College, Dublin. His eighth collection, *The Weather in Japan* (2000), won the T.S. Eliot Prize and the Hawthornden Prize. He was awarded the Queen's Gold Medal for Poetry in 2001, and his *Collected Poems* was published in 2006. He was Professor of Poetry for Ireland 2007–10. His new collection, *The Stairwell*, is published in 2014.

Peter McCarey, a Glasgow poet living in Geneva, studied Russian language and literature at Oxford, Glasgow, Leningrad and Bradford. He runs the language service of the World Health Organization. His work is published in *Collected Contraptions* (2011), *Find an Angel and Pick a Fight* (2013) and The Syllabary (www.thesyllabary.com and www.knot.ch).

Tom Pow, poet and creative writing tutor, has visited Russia on a number of occasions, most recently in connection with his book *In Another World: Among Europe's Dying Villages* (2011). He developed an interest in the *chastushka* at that time. Poems borrowing from and based on *chastushkas* were published in the chapbook *Songs from a Dying Village* (2009).

Tessa Ransford is a poet, translator, literary editor and cultural activist (www.wisdomfield.com). She was the founding director of the Scottish Poetry Library, and in 2001 initiated the annual

Callum Macdonald Memorial Award for publishers of pamphlet poetry in Scotland. Recent publications include *Not Just Moonshine: New and Selected Poems* (2008) and, with Iyad Hayatleh, *Rug of a Thousand Colours* (Arabic and English poems).

Alan Riach is the Professor of Scottish Literature at Glasgow University, author of *Representing Scotland in Literature, Popular Culture and Iconography* (2005) and co-author with Alexander Moffat of *Arts of Resistance: Poets, Portraits and Landscapes of Modern Scotland* (2009). His fifth book of poems is *Homecoming: New Poems 2001–2009* (2009), and he has also translated Duncan Ban McIntyre's *Praise of Ben Dorain*.

Christopher Rush, who taught English at George Watson's College in Edinburgh for 30 years, has written in most genres as poet, novelist, biographer, memoirist and translator into both English and Scots. His contribution has been recognised by the University of Aberdeen, which recently conferred on him the honorary degree of Doctor of Letters.

Anna Rush taught English at the University of Vladimir and received her PhD from the University of St Andrews. She has taught Russian language and literature at George Watson's College and at the University of St Andrews. A freelance translator, she translated Yury Tynyanov's novel *Pushkin* (2007), and is working on translations of Tynyanov's *Wax Effigy* and Victor Erofeev's *The Good Stalin*.

Rab Wilson lives in Ayrshire, Scotland. He writes predominantly in the Scots language and has 'owerset' (translated) works of global literature and poetry into Scots, including *The Ruba'iyat of Omar Khayyam* and Horace's First Book of *Satires*. He is a council member of the Scots Language Centre. His most recent collection of poetry is *A Map for the Blind* (2011).